WILLIAMS
SONOMA
CALIFORNIA

DRINKS FOR EVERY SEASON

150+ Recipes for
Cocktails & Nonalcoholic Drinks
Throughout the Year

PHOTOGRAPHY BY ERIN SCOTT

weldon**owen**

CONTENTS

It's Happy Hour	6
Build a Bar	9
Garnishes Galore	10
Essential Bar Tools	12
On the Rocks	15
Terms & Techniques	16

SPRING

St-Germain Greyhound	20
London Cocktail	22
Songbird	23
Pegu Cocktail	25
A Meadow for Eeyore	26
The Final Four	27
Blackberry-Thyme Bellini	28
Faux-Loma	30
Rosita Spritz	31
Ginger Gin Rickey	33
El Chupacabra	34
The Spring Solar	35
Rosé & Roses	36
Brandy Crusta	38
Strawberry-Lillet Vodka Soda	39
Rhubarb Spritz	41
Rhubarb Shrub	42
Cucumber Elderflower Fizz	43
Mai Tai	44
Classic Sazerac	45
Strawberry Basil Gin & Tonic	46
Grapefruit Beer Bellini	47
Coconut Cream & Lime Margarita	48
Mint Julep	50
Basil Julep	51

SUMMER

Champagne Cobbler	54
Peach-Basil Mimosa	56
Blackberry Lemonade Whiskey Sour	57
Saint Tiki	59
Raspberry Gin Fizz	60
Summer Cup	61
Tequila Sunrise with Pineapple & Jalapeño	62
Lychee & Lime Sake Cocktail	64
Lemongrass Last Word	65
Ancho Mezcalita	67
Clover Club	68
Pineapple Julep	69
The Hummingbird	70
Watermelon Juice	71
Solstice Spritz	72
Spicy Yuzu Fizz	74
Spiked Arnold Palmer	75
Rum-Spiked Horchata	76
Smooth Criminal	77
Peanut Butter & Whiskey Milkshake	79
Nine-Botanical Bramble	80
Morning Glory	81
Honeybee Fizz	82
Beer Margarita	83
Watermelon Tequila Punch	84
Carrot, Ginger & Tequila Punch	86
Amaretto Sour	87

FALL

Pomegranate Apple Spiced Cider	90
Americano	92
Sherry Flip	93
Apple & Honey Bee's Knees	95
The Boulevardier	96
Tea Punch	97
Bourbon Maple Fizz	98
Sparkling Corpse Reviver	100
Scotch Manhattan	101
Pomme d'Amour	102
In Full Fig	103
Blood Orange Tequila Tropi-Cal	105
Smoky Pumpkin	106

Cardamom Apple Pie	107		ANYDAY CLASSICS & TWISTS	
Persimmon Cinnamon Tea	108		Daiquiri	156
Salted Caramel Coffee	109		Raspberry-Peach Frozen Daiquiri	156
Apple Ginger Whiskey Sour	110		Thai Daiquiri	157
Brandied Mocha Coffee	112		Bloody Mary	157
Kir Royal	113		Bloody Maria with Mezcal	159
Sunset in the Garden	114		Old-Fashioned	159
Chai-Spiced Hot Toddy	115		Manhattan	160
Mamacita (Mezcal Side Car)	117		Hibiscus & Tart Cherry Manhattan	160
Good Morning Grey	118		Brandy Alexander	160
Mezcal Sour	119		Classic Negroni	161
			Not Your Negroni	161
WINTER			Frozen Orange Negroni	161
Wild Mule	122		Oaxacan Negroni	162
Baltimore Eggnog	124		Tarragon Negroni	162
Persimmon Nog	125		Margarita	162
Gingerbread Dark & Stormy	127		Mojito	163
New York Sour	128		Mock Mojito	163
Classic Paloma	129		Rosemary-Ginger Mojito	165
Stout Sangaree	130		Gimlet	165
Tom & Jerry	131		Cucumber-Basil Gimlet	166
Hot Buttered Rum	132		Grapefruit & Sage Gimlet	166
Hot Buttered Yum	133		Cosmopolitan	166
Pining Away	134		Blood Orange Cosmopolitan	167
Brandy Lift	136		Sangria	167
Black Velvet	137		Mock Sangria	168
Mulled Winter Punch	138		Rosé & Peach Sangria	168
Citrus & Spice Mulled Wine	139		Michelada	169
Coffee Cocktail	140		Irish Coffee	169
Ice Coffee Mocktail	141		Salted Caramel Irish Coffee	170
Winter Spiced Hibiscus	143		Piña Colada	170
Bourbon & Coffee Cocktail	144		Black Russian	170
Highland Holiday Cocktail	145		White Russian	171
Caffè Corretto	146		Peppermint White Russian	171
Hot Chocolate & Peppermint			Dry Martini	171
Schnapps	147		Devon's Dirty Martini	172
Turmeric, Apple & Ginger Chai	148		Flipped Martini	172
Vanilla-Citrus Old-Fashioned	149		Ramos Gin Fizz	174
Mexican Hot Chocolate	150		Metropole	174
Warming Milk	151		Grasshopper	175
Apple Hot Toddy	152			
Apple-Bourbon Hot Toddy	153			
Spiked Peppermint Bark			*Basics*	176
Hot Chocolate	155		*Index*	182

IT'S HAPPY HOUR!

What's more satisfying than sipping on a perfectly mixed cocktail? A fizzy gin-and-citrus drink on a brisk spring day, a fruity farmers' market mocktail on a warm summer evening, a heady apple-bourbon drink on an autumn afternoon, or a warming and spicy punch on a cold winter night—whatever the season or occasion, cocktails turn any gathering into a festive one.

From choosing the right glass or garnish to demystifying bartending lingo, the advice in this volume guides you through the tips of the trade and explains which tools you'll need to master the art of mixology at home. Learn the formula for crafting the perfect cocktail with more than 150 recipes that marry modernity with tradition. Make use of the extra spring rhubarb harvest with a fruity Rhubarb Spritz (page 41), or make a big bowl of Watermelon Tequila Punch (page 84) for your next summer fête. Hunker down on cold fall days with a Salted Caramel Coffee (page 109), or toast the new year with a woodsy glass of Pining Away (page 134). And no cocktail book would be complete without a handy chapter on classic cocktails (page 156), including variations and nonalcoholic versions of quintessential drinks, such as the nonalcoholic Faux-Loma (page 30) and the Wild Mule (page 122).

A world of inspired flavor combinations puts a playful spin on our favorite cocktails and brings a fresh, contemporary profile to new classics. This collection of timeless recipes, paired with our guides, tips, and tricks, turn any casual gathering into a fun and elevated home-bar experience. With this inspiring handbook at hand, you'll be whipping up the perfect libation for every occasion, mood, and season.

SANTÉ! YUM SENG! CHEERS!

BUILD A BAR

New to the home-bar scene? Check out this handy list of bar staples to kick off your collection. If you're looking to elevate your bar game, snag a few of the more esoteric spirits below. Whether you're a beginner or seasoned veteran, having a supply of fresh herbs, citrus fruits, and prepped ice cubes on hand will take your mixology to the next level.

BASICS

Vodka

Gin

Rum

Tequila

Bourbon

Rye

Blended Scotch

Small bottle
sweet vermouth

Small bottle
dry vermouth

Angostura bitters

Peychaud's bitters

Orange bitters

Triple sec

Maraschino liqueur

Benedictine liqueur

SODAS

Cola

Fruit sodas
(such as grapefruit,
lemon-lime, etc.)

Club

Seltzer

Ginger beer

Ginger ale

Tonic

MIXERS

Tonic syrup

Bloody Mary mix

Simple syrups
(Orgeat,
Simple Syrup, etc.)

Grenadine

Fruit shrubs

EXTRAS

Mezcal

Green Chartreuse

Lillet blanc

Absinthe

Cognac

Dark rum

Light rum

Campari

ESSENTIAL BAR TOOLS

These indispensable tools will set you up with everything you need for your home bar—and to bartend with ease and success.

JUICERS

Essential for preparing drinks with fresh citrus, juicers come in many shapes and sizes. A handheld citrus squeezer is great for lemons and limes, while a citrus reamer is ideal for bigger citrus fruits like grapefruits and oranges. Juicers work well for both fruits and vegetables.

JIGGER

This small liquid measurement tool comes in both an hourglass shape and a small measuring cup style— the former is best for speed, the latter for precision.

MUDDLER

Use this baseball bat–shaped tool for crushing fruits, herbs, and sugar cubes. Look for ones made of solid wood with a flat head and long enough to clear the edge of the glass.

BAR SPOON

This long-handled spoon is also known as a cocktail or mixing spoon. It is used to stir drinks in a pitcher or shaker, or for crushing sugar, fruits, or herb leaves.

CHANNEL KNIFE

The v-shaped blade on this stout bar knife cuts long thin strips of citrus for use as a garnish.

SHAKER

No bar would be complete without this iconic tool that serves the double function of mixing and chilling. A cocktail shaker quickly and effectively cools down and mixes cocktail ingredients, but it also develops texture in the finished drink.

Boston Shaker: A two-part shaker consisting of a pint glass or metal cup and metal canister. Place ingredients in the pint glass or cup, secure the metal canister firmly on top to create a seal, then turn and shake. Strain the drink from the metal canister into a glass.

Cobbler Shaker: A three-part shaker with a built-in strainer and snug-fitting top.

STRAINER

This useful addition to your home bar keeps ice and other solid ingredients inside a shaker when you're pouring the cocktail into a glass.

Hawthorne Strainer: The coiled springs around the rim of this basic cocktail strainer ensure a snug fit with most canisters and glasses, making it a good choice for either shaken or stirred drinks.

Julep Strainer: The round, perforated bowl of this cocktail strainer looks like an oversize slotted spoon and works well for stirred drinks.

MARTINI GLASS

Use this James Bond—worthy glass for any drink served "up" (chilled, then strained).

Cocktail pairing: Pegu Cocktail (page 25)

ROCKS GLASS

Also known as an old-fashioned glass, this short and stocky tumbler is used primarily for drinks

served on the rocks (over ice).

Cocktail pairing: Pining Away (page 134)

HIGHBALL

This tall glass keeps bubbles intact, so it's perfect for drinks with carbonation served over ice.

Cocktail pairing: Strawberry-Lillet Vodka Soda (page 39)

COLLINS GLASS

Taller and narrower than a highball glass, this glass is named for the Tom Collins cocktail and is ideal when a tall and frosty glass is desired.

Cocktail pairing: Brandy Lift (page 136)

COUPE GLASS

The shallow, broad bowl of this design is ideal for shaken or stirred cocktails that are strained into a glass with no ice.

Cocktail pairing: Tarragon Negroni (page 162)

CHAMPAGNE FLUTE

The tall, slender bowl of this romantic glass showcases and preserves the effervescence of any sparkling drink.

Cocktail pairing: Blackberry-Thyme Bellini (page 28)

JULEP CUP

Although this gleaming silver cup is designed for mint juleps, it works well with any drink that has crushed ice, as the metal material helps to keep the drink cold.

Cocktail pairing: Basil Julep (page 51)

COPPER MUG

This elegant mug is typically used for Moscow mules, but is well suited for any drink with ice and soda.

Cocktail pairing: Wild Mule (page 122)

PUNCH BOWL

This big glass or other nonreactive bowl is great for entertaining, especially large parties.

Cocktail pairing: Watermelon Tequila Punch (page 84)

ON THE ROCKS

Ice is to cocktails what heat is to food—this element elevates every drink, depending on how you use it. That said, the size, shape, and amount you use can affect the taste of the drink—larger cubes melt slowly, preserving the flavors with less water dilution, while crushed ice melts quickly but guarantees a frosty glass. Adding berries, sprigs of herbs, or edible flowers to your unfrozen ice trays can also add an haute, subtle touch to your concoctions.

GARNISHES GALORE

Use garnishes to layer fresh and herbaceous flavors to any drink—and add your own signature flair. Citrus zest, mint, and fruits and berries are great to have on hand, but you can experiment with other additions: edible flowers, pickled vegetables, and salt rims are a good start.

TERMS & TECHNIQUES

Want to speak the lingo to back up your bartender skills? Master this list of common terms and never be stumped by a guest's request again.

BACK

A chaser, usually a short pour of soda, beer, or other liquid (like pickle juice)—or even some kind of snack. The back either complements the flavors of whatever is being chased or washes away the taste (not a good sign).

CALL

To ask for. When you order a drink and ask for a particular spirit, you call for it.

DRY

Low in sweetness, often used to order a martini with very little vermouth.

LONG

A drink served in a tall glass. You can sometimes request drinks that come with soda mixers to be served long with extra mixer.

NEAT

Liquor served in a glass without ice and at room temperature, usually when you are enjoying, expensive spirit. Differs from a shot in that it is served in a short (old-fashioned or rocks) glass and meant to be sipped.

(ON THE) ROCKS

A drink served in a short glass with ice. Rocks are ice cubes.

TWIST

The peel of a citrus fruit, often twisted near the drink to express the fragrant oils before being added to the drink.

UP

A drink served in a coupe or cocktail glass with no ice but always chilled.

WELL/RAIL LIQUOR

The house brands of liquor used to make a majority of the drinks. Asking for something that sits on the backbar (not in the well) is often a premium call (and costs more money).

FLAME

When bartenders set their drinks or garnishes on fire. By flaming ingredients like citrus peels, the fire caramelizes the peel and adds a smoky note to the overall aroma of the cocktail

SPRING

ST-GERMAIN GREYHOUND

The warm floral notes of St-Germain soften the tart nature of this traditional greyhound without compromising its bright, refreshing taste. Dampen the glass rim with grapefruit and coat it with salt and St-Germain Greyhound becomes a Salty Dog.

4 oz (125 ml) fresh grapefruit juice

2 oz (60 ml) vodka

1 oz (30 ml) St-Germain liqueur

1 grapefruit slice, for garnish

In a cocktail shaker filled with ice, combine the grapefruit juice, vodka, and St-Germain. Cover, shake vigorously, and strain into an ice-filled highball glass. Garnish with the grapefruit slice.

MAKES 1 COCKTAIL

LONDON COCKTAIL

This heady cocktail is given a frisson of danger by the inclusion of both gin and absinthe, the latter banned in France in 1914 (and in many other countries around the same time). By the twentieth century, absinthe in France was like gin in England in the seventeenth century: widely available, often of dubious quality, highly alcoholic, drunk mainly by the poor, and blamed for everything from epilepsy to murder.

½ **barspoon orange bitters**

½ **barspoon Simple Syrup (page 176)**

½ **barspoon absinthe**

1 oz (30 ml) dry gin

Combine all the ingredients in a mixing glass and stir well. Serve in a cocktail or Nick and Nora glass.

MAKES 1 COCKTAIL

SONGBIRD

Inspired by a visit to Copper & Kings distillery in Kentucky, where each still is named after a Bob Dylan song and music is played in the barrel-aging warehouse to agitate the brandy, barman Jason Faust developed this cocktail that blends American, Italian, and French liqueurs to toast an old flame.

1½ oz (45 ml) aged brandy, preferably Copper & Kings preferred

¾ oz (20 ml) Yellow Chartreuse

¾ oz (20 ml) Cynar

2 dashes grapefruit bitters

Lemon twist, for garnish

Combine all the ingredients except for the lemon peel in a mixing glass, add ice, and stir 20–30 seconds. Strain the cocktail into a brandy snifter or a rocks glass (or an old-fashioned glass). Express the lemon twist over the drink and drop it into the glass.

MAKES 1 COCKTAIL

PEGU COCKTAIL

This cocktail was named for the Pegu Club, a British men's club once located just outside Rangoon, Burma (today Yangon, Myanmar).

2 oz (60 ml) gin

¾ oz (20 ml) Cointreau

½ oz (15 ml) fresh lime juice

¼ oz (7 ml) fresh orange juice

3 dashes Angostura bitters

2 dashes orange bitters

1 lime slice, for garnish

In a cocktail shaker filled with ice, combine the gin, Cointreau, lime juice, orange juice, Angostura bitters, and orange bitters. Cover, shake vigorously, and strain into a chilled martini glass. Garnish with the lime slice.

MAKES 1 COCKTAIL

A MEADOW FOR EEYORE

The woodsy flavors from the herbal vermouth, chamomile, and honey in this drink are so evocative of a lovely rolling meadow that it would brighten up even Winnie the Pooh's glum companion.

1½ oz (45 ml) Imbue Petal & Thorn vermouth

½ oz (15 ml) Rich Simple Syrup (page 176)

1 teaspoon chamomile tincture (see note)

3 oz (90 ml) tonic water

Lime slice, for garnish

Seasonal edible flower or flowering herb sprig, for garnish

Add the vermouth, simple syrup, and tincture to a rocks or an old-fashioned glass, and top with tonic water. Give the mixture a gentle, quick stir with a barspoon and garnish with the lime slice and, for an extra flourish, an edible flower or sprig.

MAKES 1 COCKTAIL

LIBATION NOTE: To make a tincture, fill a small jar halfway with high-proof vodka. Add your ingredients of choice (if using spices, toast them first), close the lid, and shake the jar to combine. Place in a cool, dark location, and give the jar a shake every day or so, checking on the intensity and aroma. Don't be afraid to wait longer if it's not strong enough after a couple of weeks. Chiles might only take days, while spices could take weeks. Once the desired strength is reached, remove the solids with a tea strainer. Pour the liquid into an eyedropper or bitters bottle for maximum control.

THE FINAL FOUR

The Final Four is a nice, light, and barely sweetened drink built with layers of flavor from the four different aspects of orange extracted in the tincture. The burned orange gives the combination richness and depth.

1¼ oz (37 ml) vodka

¼ oz (7 ml) Triple Orange Tincture (page 179)

¼ oz (7 ml) Dolin Véritable Génépy des Alpes (an herbal vermouth)

Seltzer water, to top

Orange twist, for garnish

In a rocks or an old-fashioned glass with ice, add the vodka, Triple Orange Tincture, and Génépy, then top with seltzer water. Pinch the orange twist just above the drink (with the skin side facing the drink), then float it on top as a garnish.

MAKES 1 COCKTAIL

BLACKBERRY-THYME BELLINI

Originally a mix of peach purée and Champagne, this classic Italian cocktail from Harry's Bar in Venice has taken on numerous flavor infusions since its inception in 1948. The contemporary addition of blackberry and thyme lives up to the cocktail's stylish beginnings.

3 oz (90 ml) Blackberry-Thyme Syrup (page 176)

1½ oz (45 ml) Thyme Simple Syrup (page 176)

1 bottle (750 ml) chilled prosecco or other sparkling wine

6 fresh blackberries, for garnish

6 thyme sprigs, for garnish

In each of 6 Champagne flutes, combine ½ oz (15 ml) blackberry-thyme syrup and ¼ oz (7 ml) thyme simple syrup. Top off each flute with 4 oz (125 ml) of the prosecco. Garnish each Bellini with 1 blackberry and 1 thyme sprig.

MAKES 6 COCKTAILS

LIBATION NOTE: To achieve a pretty ombre effect, pour the thyme simple syrup into the flutes and fill with the prosecco, then add the blackberry-thyme syrup.

FAUX-LOMA

This mock Paloma swaps the tequila for grapefruit juice. Using grapefruit-flavored Jarritos, a Mexican soda, gives a nod to the base of Mexican liquor found in the classic cocktail.

2 oz (60 ml) fresh grapefruit juice

1 oz (30 ml) fresh lime juice

1 oz (30 ml) Simple Syrup (page 176)

Soda water or grapefruit soda, to top

Lime wedge, for garnish

In a cocktail shaker, combine the grapefruit juice, lime juice, and simple syrup. Add ice, cover, and shake vigorously for 8–10 seconds. Strain into a Collins or highball glass with ice. Top with soda water (or grapefruit soda, if using) and garnish with the lime wedge.

MAKES 1 COCKTAIL

ROSITA SPRITZ

This simple, sophisticated cocktail features Lillet Rosé, a floral rosé liqueur that's worth having in your liquor cabinet because it's also great on its own, straight or on ice.

1 oz (30 ml) mezcal reposado	1 oz (30 ml) prosecco
1 oz (30 ml) Lillet Rosé	Orange twist, for garnish

In a mixing glass with ice, stir together all the ingredients except for the orange twist until cold and well blended. Strain into a cocktail glass. Garnish with the orange twist.

MAKES 1 COCKTAIL

GINGER GIN RICKEY

A member of the fizz family of mixed drinks, rickeys are made with a base spirit, fresh lime juice, and club soda and are garnished with a wedge of lime. This gin version is the most popular drink in the fizz category, and it makes a very refreshing quaff for a warm spring day.

2 oz (60 ml) gin

1 oz (15 ml) ginger syrup (page 110)

1 oz (30 ml) fresh lime juice

5–6 oz (160–180 ml) club soda, chilled

Lime wedge, for garnish

Sliced fresh ginger, for garnish

Pour the gin, ginger syrup, and lime juice into an ice-filled Collins glass. Add the club soda and stir briefly. Garnish with the lime wedge and the sliced ginger.

MAKES 1 COCKTAIL

LIBATION NOTE: You'll notice this recipe uses no sweetener of any kind, making it a very dry drink that puts the focus on the spirit and little else. If it's too much, add some sweetener to make something more like the Raspberry Gin Fizz (page 60)

EL CHUPACABRA

Based on the vodka-based Greyhound and named after a mythical beast from Latin America, this drink is so refreshing that you might even forget about the blood-sucking spiky creature the drink is named for.

2 oz (60 ml) mezcal joven

3 oz (90 ml) fresh
grapefruit juice

2 dashes Amargo-Vallet Bitters or
Angostura Aromatic Bitters

2 lime wedges

In a cocktail shaker with ice, combine the mezcal, grapefruit juice, and bitters. Cover and shake vigorously until cold and well blended. Double-strain into a Collins glass over ice. Squeeze in lime juice to taste, and garnish with the remaining lime wedge.

MAKES 1 COCKTAIL

THE SPRING SOLAR

Most mezcals are considered "joven," or unaged, and they give cocktails a smoky, nuanced flavor profile. By contrast, "reposado" mezcal, typically aged in oak barrels for up to a year, has a smoother, less smoky flavor. "Añejo" mezcal is the oldest mezcal, aged anywhere from thirteen months to three years in oak barrels that often mask most of the agave flavor.

1½ oz (45 ml) mezcal joven, preferably Ilegal

½ oz (15 ml) Spring 44 Old Tom Gin

1 oz (30 ml) fresh lemon juice

¾ oz (20 ml) Simple Syrup (page 176)

2 dashes orange bitters

Soda water, to top

Dehydrated lemon or lemon twist, for garnish

In a cocktail shaker with ice, combine the mezcal, gin, lemon juice, simple syrup, and bitters. Cover and shake vigorously until cold and well blended. Double-strain into a Collins glass over ice. Top with the soda water. Garnish with the dehydrated lemon.

MAKES 1 COCKTAIL

ROSÉ AND ROSES

Take a pass on the tired bouquet of roses and go for this floral, light cocktail instead. The liquor takes this cocktail to the next level with deep, round flavor profiles that amplify the other ingredients, but if you've got more on the docket than drinking, you can omit the liquor for a low-ABV drink instead.

4 oz (125 ml) tequila, gin, or vodka

1 oz (30 ml) Simple Syrup (page 176)

½ oz (15 ml) rose water

½ oz (15 g) dehydrated strawberries, plus more for garnish

4 oz (125 ml) sparkling rosé

Place two coupe glasses or Champagne flutes in the freezer. In a cocktail shaker filled with ice, combine the tequila, simple syrup, rose water, and strawberries and shake until chilled, about 30 seconds. Divide the mixture evenly between the frosted glasses or flutes and top with sparkling rosé. Crush one or two dehydrated strawberries to garnish.

MAKES 2 COCKTAILS

BRANDY CRUSTA

Perfected in New Orleans in the 1850s, this drink was not known outside of the area until Jerry Thomas included it in his 1887 edition of *The Bar-Tender's Guide*. The look of the drink, with a coil of lemon peel nested in the glass and a rim frosted with sugar, made it as irresistible then as it is today.

Sugar, for rimming glass

Lemon wedge, plus 1 lemon

2 oz (60 ml) brandy

½ barspoon orange liqueur,
such as curaçao or triple sec

1 barspoon fresh lemon juice

1 barspoon gum syrup (see note)

2 dashes Angostura bitters
or other aromatic bitters

On a small plate, spread an even layer of sugar. Gently rub the lemon wedge around the rim of a chilled wine glass or coupe. Holding the base of the glass, dip the rim into the sugar. Set the glass aside.

Using a vegetable peeler, cut the peel from the whole lemon in a continuous wide strip, coil the strip, and slip it into the prepared glass. It will uncoil to almost fill the glass. This is called a horse's neck twist. Set aside. In a cocktail shaker, combine the brandy, orange liqueur, lemon juice, gum syrup, and bitters. Add ice, cover, and shake for 8–10 seconds. Strain into the prepared glass.

MAKES 1 COCKTAIL

LIBATION NOTE: Gum syrup is a rich simple syrup, which means it has a ratio of two parts sugar to one part water, with the addition of gum arabic. The gum arabic is an edible stabilizer and thickener, bestowing a velvety richness to cocktails.

STRAWBERRY-LILLET VODKA SODA

The vodka soda is a bartender's dream: vodka, soda, and ice, and that's it. But it can also be kind of boring. This recipe freshens up that familiar order, introducing muddled strawberries and Lillet, a fruity fortified wine, and gives everything a good shake.

4 fresh strawberries, sliced

½ oz (15 ml) Simple Syrup (page 176)

½ oz (15 ml) fresh lime juice

1½ oz (45 ml) vodka

1 oz (30 ml) Lillet Blanc

2 oz (60 ml) club soda

1 lime wedge,
for garnish

Reserve 1 strawberry slice for a garnish. In a cocktail shaker, muddle the remaining strawberries, simple syrup, and lime juice until the strawberries are crushed. Add the vodka, Lillet, and ice. Cover, shake vigorously, and strain into an ice-filled Collins or highball glass. Top with the club soda. Garnish with the lime wedge and reserved strawberry slice.

MAKES 1 COCKTAIL

RHUBARB SPRITZ

Tired of rhubarb pies, cobblers, and galettes? You can also take advantage of rhubarb season by incorporating rhubarb into a fizzy, refreshing cocktail! It uses rhubarb syrup, which can be used as a simple syrup to elevate herbaceous liquors like gin and sweeter liquors like bourbon.

3 oz (90 ml) sparkling prosecco or brut rosé

2 oz (60 ml) club soda

1–1½ oz (30–45 ml) Rhubarb Syrup, to taste (page 178)

½ oz (15 ml) dry vermouth

1½ oz (45 ml) gin

½ vanilla bean or rhubarb peel, for garnish

Fill a wine glass with ice and add the prosecco and club soda. Stir in the Rhubarb Syrup, vermouth, and gin. Garnish with the half of vanilla bean, split, or the rhubarb peel.

MAKES 1 COCKTAIL

RHUBARB SHRUB

Fresh rhubarb is a sure sign of spring, and this tangy cocktail made with Aperol, rhubarb shrub, and strawberry purée is a delicious "dessert in a glass" that celebrates the season.

3 tablespoons rosato vermouth

1 tablespoon Aperol

1 teaspoon Rhubarb Fruit Shrub (page 178)

1 tablespoon strawberry purée

1 teaspoon fresh lemon juice

Dash of rhubarb bitters

Fresh strawberries and blueberries, for garnish

1 mint sprig, for garnish

Confectioners' sugar, for garnish

In a cocktail shaker filled with ice, combine the vermouth, Aperol, shrub, purée, lemon juice, and bitters. Cover, shake well, and strain into a stemmed glass filled with crushed ice. Garnish with the berries and mint. Sprinkle with the sugar.

MAKES 1 COCKTAIL

CUCUMBER ELDERFLOWER FIZZ

Fresh and crisp with a hint of tropical flavors, this mocktail pairs perfectly with a warm spring day. If using a cucumber picked up from a grocery store, be sure to give it a good scrub—most grocery-store cucumbers have a layer of wax over their skin to prevent bruising and moisture loss.

3 cucumber slices

1 oz (30 ml) elderflower syrup

2 oz (60 ml) fresh lime juice

2 oz (60 ml) water

Tonic water, to top

Thin cucumber strip, for garnish

Using a muddler or the back of a spoon, muddle the cucumber slices in a cocktail shaker. Add the syrup, lime juice, water, and ice, cover, and shake well. Double-strain into a rocks glass filled with fresh ice. Top with tonic water and garnish with the cucumber strip.

MAKES 1 COCKTAIL

MAI TAI

The Mai Tai we know and love today was invented in Oakland, California, in 1944 (it's true; naysayers, begone!) by Trader Vic. The name comes from a Tahitian phrase, mai tai roa, which loosely translates to "out of this world." As the story goes, Trader Vic had some friends from Tahiti at his bar and named the drink after their reaction to the first sip.

1 oz (30 ml) Jamaican rum (like Appleton Estate 12 Year)

1 oz (30 ml) Denizen Merchant's Reserve rum

¾ oz (20 ml) fresh lime juice

½ oz (15 ml) dry curaçao

½ oz (15 ml) orgeat almond syrup

¼ oz (7 ml) Simple Syrup (page 176)

Lime slice, for garnish

Mint sprig, for garnish

In a cocktail shaker, combine all the ingredients except for the mint and the lime wheel. Add ice, cover, and shake vigorously for 8–10 seconds. Strain into a cold glass. Garnish with the lime slice and mint sprig.

MAKES 1 COCKTAIL

CLASSIC SAZERAC

Though this is the formula for a classic Sazerac, for an old-school twist, swap out the whiskey for Cognac—you'll get a real taste of the 1850s.

1 demerara sugar cube

3 dashes Peychaud's bitters

2 oz (60 ml) rye whiskey

¼ oz (7 ml) Herbsaint
or absinthe

Lemon twist, for garnish

Fill an old-fashioned or a rocks glass with ice and set aside. In a pint or mixing glass, add the sugar cube and soak it with Peychaud's bitters, then muddle. Add the rye whiskey, and ice, then stir until the sugar is dissolved. Remove the ice from the glass, pour in the Herbsaint or absinthe, and swirl to coat the glass. Strain the cocktail from the mixing or pint glass into the prepared glass. Express the lemon twist over the drink and drop it into the glass..

MAKES 1 COCKTAIL

STRAWBERRY BASIL GIN & TONIC

We used Hendricks Gin here for the strong floral notes in the liquor. Lighter elements, like the cucumber and the basil, won't get lost among the strong herbal notes that other gins contain, and the flowery taste makes the strawberry the star of the show.

Cucumber, thinly sliced, to serve

2 oz (60 ml) gin, such as Hendricks

3 fresh strawberries, halved

1 fresh basil leaf

6 oz (180 ml) tonic water

Line a chilled balloon glass with the cucumber and set aside. In a cocktail shaker, combine the gin, strawberries, basil, and ice. Cover and shake for 10 seconds. Fill the glass with a 1 large ice cube and tonic. Double-strain the drink over the ice.

MAKES 1 COCKTAIL

LIBATION NOTE: Ice melts at a slower rate in a balloon glass, keeping the cocktail colder and less diluted for longer. The wide shape of the glass allows you to smell more botanical flavors coming from the cocktail. The larger the ice cube, the slower it will melt, resulting in slower dilution.

GRAPEFRUIT BEER BELLINI

We used Stiegl Grapefruit Radler to make this cocktail, but you can use most grapefruit beers—try Crane Brewing's Grapefruit Gose for a sour drink, Leinenkugel's Grapefruit Shandy for something lighter and sweeter, or Boulevard Brewing's Unfiltered Grapefruit Wheat Beer for a thicker texture. Avoid grapefruit IPAs—the powerful hop profile will overwhelm the other ingredients.

2 grapefruits, peeled, seeded, and cut into wedges

1 tablespoon sugar

1 (16-oz/500-ml) can grapefruit beer such as Stiegl Grapefruit Radler

In a blender, combine the grapefruit wedges and sugar and blend on high until smooth, about 30 seconds. Divide the grapefruit purée evenly among four flute glasses. Top each with 4 oz (125 ml) grapefruit beer.

MAKES 4 COCKTAILS

COCONUT CREAM & LIME MARGARITA

Blanco tequila is a pure form of the agave-fermeneted alcohol which, unlike resposados and añejos, is not aged in wood. Here, the lightest tequila gets a rich and creamy edge from coconut cream, to which the standard mix of orange-flavored liqueur and lime juice is added.

Kosher salt, grated lime zest, and sugar for rimming glass

2 lime wedges

2 oz (60 ml) coconut cream or cream of coconut

1½ oz (45 ml) blanco tequila

1 oz (30 ml) fresh lime juice

½ oz (15 ml) Cointreau

¼ oz (7 ml) Simple Syrup (page 176)

On a small plate, combine equal parts salt, lime zest, and sugar and spread in an even layer. Gently rub 1 of the lime wedges around the rim of a rocks glass. Holding the base of the glass, dip the rim into the salt mixture. Place in the refrigerator until ready to use.

Just before serving, fill the glass with ice. In a cocktail shaker filled with ice, combine the coconut cream, tequila, lime juice, Cointreau, and simple syrup. Cover, shake vigorously, and strain into the ice-filled glass. Garnish with the remaining lime wedge.

MAKES 1 COCKTAIL

MINT JULEP

Basically a whiskey sling (a drink with spirits, sugar, and water) with crushed ice instead of water, the mint julep is the drink that launched mixology. Simple, elegant, and, most importantly, cold, it comes with an aromatic mint garnish that one inhales as one sips the sweetened bourbon.

¾ oz (20 ml) Simple Syrup (page 176)

2 oz (60 ml) bourbon whiskey

3 large mint sprigs,
for garnish

Pour the simple syrup into a julep cup or an old-fashioned glass filled with crushed ice. Stir well. Add the bourbon and stir until a film of ice forms on the exterior of the cup. Garnish with the mint sprigs.

MAKES 1 COCKTAIL

LIBATION NOTE: Juleps can be made with spirits other than bourbon. In fact, peach brandy was the earlier basis for the drink, but your favorite spirit—gin, Cognac, and even fortified wines like sherry and port—will work here, too.

BASIL JULEP

Basil stands in for the mint in this contemporary version of the Southern classic. Julep fans and Kentucky Derby—goers alike will appreciate this makeover, which mixes the pungent basil and tart lime with a top-shelf bourbon. Don't skimp on the crushed ice—it is essential to a good julep.

9 fresh basil leaves

1 oz (30 ml) Basil Simple Syrup
(page 176)

1½ oz (45 ml) bourbon

1 oz (30 ml) fresh lime juice

1 lime wedge, for garnish

In a rocks glass, muddle 8 of the basil leaves and the basil simple syrup. Add the bourbon and lime juice, pack the glass tightly with crushed ice, and stir until the glass is frosted on the outside. Top with more crushed ice to form a dome. Garnish with the remaining basil leaf and the lime wedge.

MAKES 1 COCKTAIL

SUMMER

CHAMPAGNE COBBLER

Cobblers are a style of drink from the mid-1800s that were designed, like juleps (see page 50), to cool you down in a hurry. But unlike juleps, the ice here isn't flaky and snowy. It is instead crushed to the size of small pebbles, or "cobbles."

½ oz (15 ml) Rich Simple Syrup or gum syrup (pages 176 and 38)

Sparkling wine (preferably brut)

Lemon twist and orange twist, for garnish

Mixed seasonal berries or other fruit, for garnish

Pour the simple syrup into a julep cup or double old-fashioned glass filled two-thirds full with pebble-size ice. Add the sparkling wine to the cup to fill. Express the citrus twists over the drink and drop them into the cup. Garnish with the berries. Serve with a straw.

MAKES 1 COCKTAIL

LIBATION NOTE: You can swap out the rich simple syrup for Raspberry Simple Syrup (page 176), which will accentuate the berry garnish but not dominate the drink.

PEACH-BASIL MIMOSA

A peach- and basil-infused simple syrup adds a sweet, herbal note to sparkling wine. Serve this refreshing Champagne cocktail at brunch or an outdoor summer gathering when peaches are at their peak, and drop a slice into the glass alongside the basil sprig.

6 oz (180 ml) chilled Champagne
or sparkling wine

1 oz (30 ml) Peach-Basil Syrup
(page 176)

1 basil sprig, for garnish

In a Champagne flute or coupe glass, combine 2 oz (60 ml) of the Champagne and the peach-basil syrup and stir gently. Top with the remaining Champagne and garnish with the basil sprig.

MAKES 1 COCKTAIL

BLACKBERRY LEMONADE WHISKEY SOUR

This dressed-up version of a whiskey sour adds sweet black-berry coulis to the traditional mix of whiskey, lemon juice, and sugar.

FOR THE BLACKBERRY COULIS:

4 cups (450 g) fresh blackberries

2 tablespoons fresh lemon juice

2 oz (60 ml) whiskey

1½ oz (45 ml) fresh lemon juice

1 oz (30 ml) Simple Syrup (page 176)

1 large egg white

Lemon twist, for garnish

To make the blackberry coulis, in a blender, combine the blackberries and lemon juice and blend until smooth. Strain the blackberry coulis through a fine-mesh sieve into a container. Use at once, or cover and refrigerate for up to 2 days.

In a cocktail shaker, combine the whiskey, lemon juice, simple syrup, 1 oz of the blackberry coulis, and egg white. Cover and shake vigorously, then open the shaker and add ice. Cover, shake vigorously again, and strain into a chilled rocks glass over 1 large ice cube. Garnish with the lemon twist.

MAKES 1 COCKTAIL

SAINT TIKI

Using cocktail bitters in mocktails is controversial, since they are typically alcoholic—but they are used in such small quantities that they end up contributing just trace amounts. Bitters are great for adding layers of complexity to an otherwise simple (and alcohol-free) drink. Just make sure that your guest isn't allergic or completely opposed to the idea.

2 oz (60 ml) fresh orange juice

2 oz (60 ml) pineapple juice

¾ oz (20 ml) fresh lime juice

½ oz (15 ml) Cinnamon Simple Syrup (page 176)

2 dashes Tiki bitters (optional)

Ginger beer, to top

Mint sprig, for garnish

In a cocktail shaker, combine the orange, pineapple, and lime juices, cinnamon simple syrup, and bitters, if using. Add ice, cover, and shake vigorously for 8–10 seconds. Strain into a cold coupe or cocktail glass. Top with ginger beer and garnish with the mint sprig.

MAKES 1 COCKTAIL

RASPBERRY GIN FIZZ

The fizz is a style of drink that utilizes the effervescence of club soda or seltzer water to give the drink levity and refreshing qualities and includes siblings like the Ramos Gin Fizz (page 174), Ginger Gin Rickey (page 33), and countless other variations. This version gets dressed up with raspberry syrup, a popular addition in the late nineteenth century.

2 oz (60 ml) Old Tom gin

¾ oz (20 ml) fresh lime juice

¾ oz (20 ml) Raspberry Simple Syrup (page 176)

5–6 oz (160–180 ml) club soda, chilled

Lime wedge and fresh raspberries, for garnish

In a cocktail shaker, combine the gin, lime juice, and raspberry simple syrup. Add ice, cover, and shake vigorously for 8–10 seconds. Strain into a chilled Collins glass. Add the club soda and stir briefly, then add as many ice cubes as will fit without spilling. Garnish with the lime wedge and raspberries.

MAKES 1 COCKTAIL

LIBATION NOTE: Popular in eighteenth-century England, Old Tom is a style of gin that is slightly sweet. It got its name from signs shaped like a black cat (an "old tom") displayed on pubs to signify the gin was served there.

SUMMER CUP

Also called a Pimm's Cup, this marvelously refreshing long drink was created in the 1820s by Londoner James Pimm at his restaurant. Starting from traditional English fruit cups, which were a mix of fruit, juices, spirits, and sugar, Pimm concocted a gin-based tonic, flavored with fruit liqueurs and herbs, and began selling it commercially in 1859. The company eventually developed six varieties of Pimm's, each using a different spirit—gin, scotch, brandy, rum, vodka, rye whiskey—though most of them are no longer available.

2 oz (60 ml) Pimm's No. 1

4 oz (120 ml) ginger ale

Ribbon of cucumber and orange slice (optional), for garnish

In an ice-filled Collins glass, combine the Pimm's and ginger ale and stir to mix. Garnish with the cucumber ribbon and orange slice, if using.

MAKES 1 COCKTAIL

TEQUILA SUNRISE WITH PINEAPPLE & JALAPEÑO

With its crimson to golden hue and fruity flavor, this ombre cocktail is a favorite party drink. Here, the classic mix is given a contemporary spin with muddled chile and charred pineapple. For a tequila sunset, substitute blackberry brandy for the grenadine.

2 oz (60 g) pineapple chunks

4 thin jalapeño chile slices

4 oz (125 ml) fresh orange juice

2 oz (60 ml) tequila

½ oz (15 ml) grenadine

Pat the pineapple chunks dry with a paper towel. In a small frying pan over medium-high heat, cook the pineapple, turning once, until beginning to char, about 3 minutes per side. Remove from the heat and let cool briefly. Reserve 1 chunk for a garnish. In a cocktail shaker, muddle the remaining pineapple chunks and 3 of the jalapeño slices. Add the orange juice, tequila, and ice. Cover, shake vigorously, and strain into an ice-filled highball glass. Slowly pour the grenadine over the back of a spoon into the glass. Garnish with the reserved pineapple chunk and the remaining jalapeño slice.

MAKES 1 COCKTAIL

LIBATION NOTE: The subtle infusion of jalapeño chile and caramelized pineapple adds unexpected heat and depth of flavor to this riff on the cocktail classic.

LYCHEE & LIME SAKE COCKTAIL

Rice wine is a nice, light spirit for mixing, delicately accepting the flavors of the ingredients with which it is blended. Here, it melds well with sweet lychee and tart lime for a delicious drink any day of the year.

2 oz (60 ml) sake

1 oz (30 ml) lychee syrup, strained from the can, plus 2 lychees

1 oz (30 ml) fresh lime juice

½ oz (15 ml) grenadine

In a cocktail shaker filled with ice, combine the sake, lychee syrup, lime juice, and grenadine. Cover, shake vigorously, and strain into a chilled coupe or martini glass. Garnish with the lychees.

MAKES 1 COCKTAIL

LEMONGRASS LAST WORD

Two Southeast Asian flavors—lemongrass and kaffir lime—give this sweet-sour cocktail a refreshing profile. Add equal parts of all ingredients to scale up for serving a crowd.

¾ oz (20 ml) gin

¾ oz (20 ml) Green Chartreuse

¾ oz (20 ml) Lemongrass Simple Syrup (page 176)

¾ oz (20 ml) fresh lime juice

1 Kaffir lime leaf, for garnish

1 lime wedge, for garnish

In a cocktail shaker filled with ice, combine the gin, green Chartreuse, lemongrass simple syrup, and lime juice. Cover, shake vigorously, and strain into a chilled coupe glass. Garnish with the kaffir lime leaf and lime wedge.

MAKES 1 COCKTAIL

ANCHO MEZCALITA

Ancho Reyes Ancho Chile Liqueur is a sublime addition to a mezcal cocktail. Made with dried ancho chiles steeped in a sugarcane-based spirit, it originates in Puebla, one of the newest Mexican states legally allowed to produce mezcal.

Chile powder (preferably pequin chiles) for rimming glass

Salt for rimming glass

1 lime wedge

1 oz (30 ml) mezcal joven

1 oz (30 ml) Ancho Reyes Ancho Chile Liqueur

1 oz (30 ml) fresh lime juice

½ oz (15 ml) agave nectar

Lime slice, for garnish

On a small plate, mix equal parts chile powder and salt and spread in an even layer. Gently rub the lime wedge around the rim of a rocks glass. Holding the base of the glass, dip the rim into the mixture. Set the glass aside. (The leftover mixture can be stored in an airtight jar.)

In a cocktail shaker with ice, combine the mezcal, liqueur, lime juice, and agave nectar. Cover and shake vigorously until cold and well blended. Double-strain into the glass over ice. Garnish with the lime slice.

MAKES 1 COCKTAIL

CLOVER CLUB

Developed by barman and hotelier George Boldt, who owned Philadelphia's Bellevue-Stratford Hotel, this frothy, delicate drink is named for a local men's club that met regularly at the hotel from the late 1800s to the early 1900s.

1 oz (30 ml) gin

1 oz (30 ml) dry vermouth

½ oz (15 ml) fresh lemon juice

½ oz (15 ml) egg white
(about ½ egg white)

½ oz (15 ml) Raspberry Simple Syrup (page 176)

1½ barspoons Simple Syrup (page 176)

In a cocktail shaker, combine all the ingredients, cover, and shake vigorously for 10–15 seconds so the egg white froths up and emulsifies. Fill the shaker with ice, re-cover, and shake vigorously for about 10 seconds longer. Strain into a chilled coupe glass.

MAKES 1 COCKTAIL

LIBATION NOTE: Although this drink doesn't traditionally come with more than its frothy head as a garnish, try it with a mint sprig, slapped between your hands in a clapping motion to release the aroma before dropping it into the glass.

PINEAPPLE JULEP

Despite the "julep" in the name, this drink has nothing in common with other similarly named drinks, such as the Mint Julep on page 50, but is instead a punch. A recipe for it appears in William Terrington's 1869 *Cooling Cups and Dainty Drinks*, which was the earliest British book to include recipes for cocktails as well as other popular British and European libations.

1 pineapple, peeled and chopped

4 oz (125 ml) Bols barrel-aged genever

4 oz (125 ml) maraschino liqueur

4 oz (125 ml) Raspberry Simple Syrup (page 176)

Juice of 2 oranges

1 bottle (750 ml) sparkling wine, chilled

Seasonal berries, for garnish

Combine the pineapple, genever, maraschino liqueur, raspberry simple syrup, orange juice, wine, and about 3½ (450 g) shaved or crushed ice in a punch bowl and stir to combine. Garnish with the berries. To serve, ladle into punch cups.

MAKES 4 COCKTAILS

LIBATION NOTE: If you can't find barrel-aged genever, feel free to substitute your favorite whiskey here.

THE HUMMINGBIRD

Named for the bright red nectar used in hummingbird feeders, this drink is a play on bitters and soda, enriched with vanilla and coffee. Cappelletti is less bitter than other Italian aperitivos, making for a smooth, elegant drink.

1½ oz (45 ml) Cappelletti aperitivo

1 teaspoon vanilla extract

1 teaspoon coffee tincture (page 26, use a one-part to two-parts ratio of whole coffee beans to liquid)

3 oz (90 ml) seltzer water

Long lemon twist, made with channel knife (page 38)

Add the Cappelletti, vanilla, and tincture to a rocks or an old-fashioned glass, then top with seltzer water. Give it a gentle, quick stir with a barspoon and garnish with the lemon twist.

MAKES 1 COCKTAIL

WATERMELON JUICE

Inspired by agua fresca, meaning "fresh water" in Spanish, this drink takes blended watermelon and spices it up a bit— not just with red pepper flakes, but also with the addition of lemon-lime soda.

1 tablespoon cayenne pepper for rimming glass

⅓ cup (80 g) black salt for rimming glass

1 lime wedge

¼ lb (125 g) seedless watermelon

1 teaspoon red pepper flakes

2 oz (60 ml) fresh lime juice

1 teaspoon grated lime zest

Lemon-lime soda, to top

On a small plate, mix together the cayenne pepper and salt and spread in an even layer. Gently rub the lime wedge around the rim of a tall glass. Holding the base of the glass, dip the rim into the mixture. Set the glass aside. (The leftover cayenne and salt mixture can be stored in an airtight jar.)

Using a large knife, cut off both ends off the watermelon and stand it upright. Use a sharp knife to cut the green peel and white pith away from the flesh, rotating the watermelon as you go. Cut watermelon into 2-inch chunks.

In a blender, combine all the ingredients, except for the soda, with ½ cup (125 g) ice. Pour the blended drink into the prepared glass and top with soda.

MAKES 1 COCKTAIL

SOLSTICE SPRITZ

If you're a big fan of triple sec, consider picking up a bottle of blood orange liqueur: It's got a deeper, more complex flavor profile alongside that signature citrusy flavor. It's also a fantastic digestif—perfect for sipping.

6 oz (180 ml) prosecco	1½ oz (45 ml) Campari
3 oz (90 ml) club soda	Lemon twist, for garnish
1½ oz blood orange liqueur	Blood orange slice, for garnish

Fill a wine glass with ice and pour in the prosecco and club soda first. Stir in the blood orange liqueur and Campari. Express the lemon twist over the cocktail and garnish with the blood orange slice.

MAKES 1 COCKTAIL

LIBATION NOTE: If you choose to make the spritz in a pitcher, express the lemon twist over the wine glasses and garnish with blood orange slices.

SPICY YUZU FIZZ

Yuzu is a citrus fruit that tastes like a mash-up between grapefruit and lemon. Yuzu tea, also called yuja-cha or yuja tea, is made by mixing hot water and yuja-cheong, a yuzu marmalade. You may find dehydrated yuzu blended with other flavors in tea bags, but most likely, you'll find yuzu tea in a jar at your local Asian food market.

2 tablespoons togarashi

⅓ cup (80 g) sea salt

1 lemon wedge

2 oz (60 ml) yuzu juice

4 oz (125 ml) yuzu tea, at room temperature

1 oz (30 ml) elderflower syrup

Soda water, to top

2 jalapeño chile slices, for garnish

On a small plate, mix together the togarashi and salt and spread in an even layer. Gently rub the lemon wedge around the rim of a tall or Collins glass. Holding the base of the glass, dip the rim into the togarashi and salt mixture. Set the glass aside. (The leftover togarashi and salt mixture can be stored in an airtight jar.)

In a cocktail shaker, combine the yuzu juice, yuzu tea, and syrup. Add ice, cover, and shake until chilled. Strain the drink into the prepared glass filled with fresh ice and top with soda water. Garnish with the chile slices.

MAKES 1 COCKTAIL

SPIKED ARNOLD PALMER

An Arnold Palmer is made with equal parts iced tea and lemonade and was named for the world-famous golfer who was known to order it at restaurants and clubhouses. An alcoholic version of the drink is called an "Adult Arnold Palmer" or a "Tipsy Arnold Palmer." Whatever you call it, it's a lovely summery cocktail.

⅓ cup (80 ml) iced tea, preferably homemade

⅓ cup (80 ml) Fresh Lemonade (page 180)

3 tablespoons vodka

1 lemon wedge, for garnish

1 mint sprig, for garnish

Fill a large rocks glass with ice. Add the tea, lemonade, and vodka. Stir with a long spoon. Garnish with the lemon wedge and mint sprig.

MAKES 1 COCKTAIL

RUM-SPIKED HORCHATA

Horchata is a sweet milk drink made with pulverized uncooked rice. This refreshing agua fresca is very popular in Mexico and other Latin American countries and is especially good with a healthy dose of rum.

1 lb (455 g) uncooked long-grain rice	⅓ cup (90 g) sugar
6 cups (1.5 L) cold water	1 teaspoon vanilla
Generous pinch of ground cinnamon, plus more for garnish	½ cup (125 ml) light rum
	4 cinnamon sticks, for garnish

The day before serving, soak the rice in 3 cups (750 ml) of the water overnight. Transfer the rice, soaking water, and cinnamon to a blender and purée until smooth. Strain the mixture into a pitcher through a fine-mesh sieve or several layers of cheesecloth. Add the remaining 3 cups (750 ml) of water, the sugar, and vanilla to the pitcher and stir well. Taste and adjust the flavors, if necessary.

To serve, fill four large glasses with ice and add the rum in equal parts. Pour the horchata into each glass and stir with a long spoon. Garnish each drink with the cinnamon and a cinnamon stick.

MAKES 4 DRINKS

SMOOTH CRIMINAL

Refreshing for summer, this simply perfect cocktail is by acclaimed bartender Carlos Abeyta.

1½ oz (45 ml) mezcal joven, preferably Ilegal, or anejo

½ oz (15 ml) fresh lime juice

¾ oz (20 ml) fresh lemon juice

¾ oz (20 ml) peach purée

Lemon or lime slice, for garnish

In a cocktail shaker with ice, combine all the ingredients except for the lemon or lime slice. Cover and vigorously shake until cold and well blended. Double-strain into a rocks glass over ice. Garnish with a lemon or lime slice.

MAKES 1 COCKTAIL

PEANUT BUTTER & WHISKEY MILKSHAKE

Skip the drive-thru shakes and make yourself one of these PB&W treats! Many companies are jumping on the peanut butter whiskey bandwagon: try Screwball Peanut Butter Whiskey, Old Oak Five O'Clock Peanut Butter Whiskey or John A.P. Conoley Carolina Peanut Butter Flavored Whiskey.

¼ cup (60 ml) whole milk, plus more as needed

4 cups (680 g) vanilla bean ice cream

½ cup (125 ml) Screwball Peanut Butter Whiskey, plus more as desired

4 tablespoons (70 g) creamy peanut butter, plus more for garnish

Pinch salt

Chocolate syrup to taste, plus more for garnish

Fresh Whipped Cream (page 179), for garnish

Chopped peanuts, for garnish

In a blender, combine the milk, ice cream, whiskey, peanut butter, salt, and chocolate syrup. Blend on high until the mixture is smooth, adding slightly more milk if the texture is too thick.

Spread peanut butter on the rims of two tall milkshake glasses, then drizzle chocolate sauce on the interior of the glasses. Divide the milkshake mixture evenly between the prepared glasses. If desired, top each milkshake with a ½ oz (15 ml) shooter of the peanut butter whiskey. Top the milkshakes with whipped cream and chopped peanuts.

MAKES 2 COCKTAILS

NINE-BOTANICAL BRAMBLE

Using crushed ice in a drink doesn't just make it look cool, it also turns your drink into an evolving experience. That's because as the ice dilutes the cocktail, the flavor of the drink changes. Additionally, you'll begin to smell the garnish more—in this case, basil and blackberry. If you don't have a crushed ice machine, go pick some up at a fast-food restaurant. Or put some ice in a bag and smash it with a hammer. This original crushed-ice cocktail showcases Pierde Almas's +9 Botanical Mezcal, which is infused with juniper berries and other botanicals typically used in making gin.

2 oz (60 ml) Pierde Almas +9 Botanical Mezcal

¾ oz (20 ml) crème de mûre (blackberry liqueur)

½ oz (15 ml) fresh lemon juice

1 barspoon or teaspoon Simple Syrup (page 176)

1–2 fresh blackberries, for garnish

1 fresh basil leaf, for garnish

In a cocktail shaker with ice, shake together all the ingredients, except for the blackberry and basil leaf, until cold and well blended. Double-strain into a snifter over crushed ice. Garnish with a blackberry and a basil leaf on a skewer.

MAKES 1 COCKTAIL

MORNING GLORY

Had a crazy night out? This cocktail is the perfect "hair of the dog" to help revive you. Although it's always best to salt the side of the glass instead of the rim, don't worry about that here: It's nice when a bit of salt falls into the drink while you're climbing back into bed. You can use a lighter beer like Modelo, but Victoria, another Mexican beer, has a bit more body to enjoy with that recovery breakfast.

Chile powder (preferably pequin chiles) for rimming glass

Salt for rimming glass

1 lime wedge

3 slices cucumber

1 oz (30 ml) mezcal reposado

½ oz (15 ml) mezcal joven

1 oz (30 ml) fresh lime juice

¼ oz (7 ml) Simple Syrup (page 176)

Beer, to top, preferably Victoria

Cucumber slices, for garnish

On a small plate, mix equal parts chile powder and salt and spread in an even layer. Gently rub the lime wedge around the rim of a pint glass. Holding the base of the glass, dip the rim into the mixture. Set the glass aside. (The leftover salt mixture can be stored in an airtight jar.)

In a cocktail shaker, muddle a cucumber. Add the mezcals, lime juice, simple syrup, and some ice. Cover and vigorously shake until cold and well blended. Double-strain the contents into the prepared glass over ice. Top with beer and garnish with a cucumber slice.

MAKES 1 COCKTAIL

HONEYBEE FIZZ

This is a perfect libation for anyone looking for an afternoon pick-me-up, with bitters that mellow out the sweetness of the cocktail. If you'd like to play up that element, swapping out the cherry for some blackberries will add a tangy tartness and complement the bitters.

2 oz (60 ml) lemon juice

1½ oz (45 ml) Rich Simple Syrup (page 176)

Soda water, to top

2 dashes Angostura bitters (optional)

Cherry, for garnish

In a Collins or highball glass with ice, add the lemon juice and simple syrup and stir. Top with soda water. Add the bitters and garnish with the cherry.

MAKES 1 COCKTAIL

BEER MARGARITA

You'll want to pay attention to the kind of beer you use for this concoction—lighter beers like Corona, Modelo, or Bud Light will serve as a tame backdrop for the stronger tequila and Cointreau. Heavy, full-flavored beers like stouts or IPAs may mask the other flavors of the drink.

Kosher salt

1 lime wedge

1½ oz (45 ml) tequila blanco
or reposado

1 oz (30 ml) Cointreau

1 oz (30 ml) fresh lime juice

¼ oz Simple Syrup (page 176)
(optional)

4 oz (125 ml) chilled beer, such as
a pale lager like Corona

Lime slice, for garnish

On a small plate, spread salt in an even layer. Gently rub the lime wedge around the rim of a glass. Holding the base of the glass, dip the rim into the salt.

Combine the tequila, Cointreau, lime juice, and simple syrup in the glass and stir to combine. Fill the glass with ice, then pour the beer over the ice. Garnish with the lime slice.

MAKES 1 COCKTAIL

WATERMELON TEQUILA PUNCH

Agave nectar is the ideal choice for this punch, because it enhances the agave flavor of the tequila, but a one-to-one swap of simple syrup will do in a pinch.

1 large 6–8 pound (3–4 kg) seedless watermelon

1½ cups (375 ml) fresh lime juice

⅓ cup (80 ml) agave nectar

2 cups (500 ml) tequila

¾ cup (180 ml) elderflower liqueur, preferably St-Germain

Lime slices, for garnish

Fresh mint leaves, for garnish

Using a large knife, cut off both ends off the watermelon and stand it upright. Use a sharp knife to cut the green peel and white pith away from the flesh, rotating the watermelon as you go. Cut watermelon into 2-inch chunks.

Transfer half the watermelon chunks to a blender and blend on high speed until smooth. Strain the blended watermelon through a fine-mesh sieve into a large bowl. Repeat with the remaining watermelon chunks. You should have about 8 cups (2 L) of watermelon purée. Add the lime juice, agave nectar, tequila, and elderflower liqueur to the bowl with the watermelon purée and stir until combined. Transfer to a punch bowl or pitcher and chill for 30 minutes. Pour into ice-filled glasses and garnish the glasses with lime slices and mint leaves.

MAKES ABOUT 12 COCKTAILS

CARROT, GINGER & TEQUILA PUNCH

You can buy carrot juice at your local grocery store, or you can opt to make it: Grab 2 pounds (1 kg) carrots, chop into ½-inch (12-mm) slices, then purée them in a blender. In a saucepan over high heat, bring water to a boil, add the carrot purée, then remove the pan from the heat. Let the mixture steep for about 20 minutes. Strain the pulp through a fine-mesh sieve, and store the liquid in an airtight container in the refrigerator for up to one week.

4 cups (1 L) carrot juice

½ cup (125 ml) fresh orange juice

¾ cup (180 ml) fresh lime juice

2 tablespoons freshly grated ginger

1½ cups (375 ml) tequila Blanco

Rosemary sprigs, for garnish

Thyme sprigs, for garnish

In a large pitcher or punch bowl, combine all the ingredients. Stir and chill for 30 minutes. Pour into ice-filled glasses and garnish with rosemary and thyme sprigs.

MAKES 8–10 COCKTAILS

AMARETTO SOUR

This not-too-sweet version of an Amaretto Sour makes a very good after-dinner drink that pairs well with chocolate.

3 tablespoons amaretto

1 tablespoon plus 1 teaspoon bourbon

2 tablespoons fresh lemon juice

1 teaspoon Simple Syrup (page 176)

1 tablespoon beaten egg white

Lemon twist, for garnish

1 marinated cherry, for garnish

Fill a cocktail shaker with cracked ice and add the amaretto, bourbon, lemon juice, simple syrup, and egg white. Cover and shake well. Strain into a rocks glass filled with ice. Garnish with the lemon twist and cherry.

MAKES 1 COCKTAIL

FALL

POMEGRANATE APPLE SPICED CIDER

Though "molasses" implies some sort of sweetening agent, pomegranate molasses is made by simply cooking pomegranate juice to a thick consistency—thus, it will retain a lot of the tartness of the fruit. The real sweetness of this drink will come from the apples, which mellow out the spices and tart flavors of this autumnal drink.

6 oz (¾ cup) nonalcoholic apple cider or apple juice

2 star anise pods

4 whole cloves

1 cardamom pod

1 cinnamon stick

1 tablespoon pomegranate molasses

In a small pan, combine the apple cider and spices and bring to a boil. Reduce the heat and simmer for 10 minutes until spices are infused. Remove from the heat, add the pomegranate molasses and stir to combine. Serve in a mug or heatproof glass.

MAKES 1 COCKTAIL

AMERICANO

Vermouths, which are wines infused with botanicals, and bitter liqueurs, such as Campari, are common ingredients in predinner drinks in Europe, so it makes sense that someone would combine the two. Like much in the bar world, there are conflicting stories about the origin of the name of the Americano: some say it comes from the Italian word *amer* (Italian for bitter), and others say it was named after Americans enjoying the drink. One thing we can agree on: it's delicious.

1 oz (30 ml) sweet vermouth

1 oz (30 ml) Campari

1½ oz (45 ml) seltzer water

Lemon or orange slice, for garnish

In a highball glass with ice, add the vermouth, Campari, and seltzer. Stir to combine and garnish with the citrus slice.

MAKES 1 COCKTAIL

SHERRY FLIP

A very old style of drink, flips call for a whole egg (sometimes just the yolk), creating a hearty, fortifying mixture that tastes much better than it sounds. Any of the dry sherries—fino, manzanilla, amontillado—work here.

2½ oz (75 ml) dry sherry

¾ oz (20 ml) Simple Syrup (page 176)

1 egg

Ground or freshly grated nutmeg, for garnish

In a cocktail shaker, combine the sherry, simple syrup, and egg. Add ice, cover, and shake vigorously for 8–10 seconds. Strain into a chilled cocktail glass, wine glass, or coupe. Sprinkle with the nutmeg.

MAKES 1 COCKTAIL

LIBATION NOTE: You can use a sweeter or heartier sherry here, such as an oloroso, for more intensity, but be sure to dial back the amount of simple syrup (or eliminate it entirely) if you use a cream sherry or anything sweetened.

APPLE & HONEY BEE'S KNEES

This modern take on the prohibition-era classic swaps out the traditional honey for sweet cinnamon-apple syrup.

1 tablespoon sugar
for rimming glass

1 teaspoon ground cinnamon
for rimming glass

1 lemon wedge

2 oz (60 ml) gin

1½ oz (45 ml) Cinnamon-
Apple Syrup (page 176)

1 oz (30 ml) fresh lemon juice

1 cinnamon stick, for garnish

1 apple slice, for garnish

On a small plate, mix together the sugar and cinnamon and spread in an even layer. Gently rub the lemon wedge around the rim of a coupe glass. Holding the base of the glass, dip the rim into the mixture. Set the glass aside.

In a cocktail shaker filled with ice, combine the gin, cinnamon-apple syrup, and lemon juice. Cover, shake vigorously, and strain into the prepared glass. Garnish with the cinnamon stick and float an apple slice on top.

MAKES 1 COCKTAIL

THE BOULEVARDIER

This Negroni variation appears in Harry MacElhone's 1927 book *Barflies and Cocktails*. It makes a nice, pleasantly bitter drink—perfect for after dinner

1 oz (30 ml) bourbon whiskey	**1 oz (30 ml) Campari**
1 oz (30 ml) sweet vermouth	**Orange twist, for garnish**

Combine all the ingredients in a mixing glass filled with ice and stir until well chilled, 20–30 seconds. Strain into a chilled cocktail glass. Express the orange twist over the drink and drop it into the glass.

MAKES 1 COCKTAIL

TEA PUNCH

Hot punches like this one were winter drinks, served at balls and at holiday celebrations such as Christmas and New Year's. The original title of the recipe was *Punch au thé à l'anglaise*, pointing out, once again, the association of the English with black tea. It comes from Alfred Suzanne's 1904 book *La Cuisine et pâtisserie anglaise et américaine*, which was aimed at French chefs aspiring to work in the United Kingdom or the United States. It purported to contain all the recipes that each nation regarded as a necessity on its tables. It was an odd claim, since in the author's view there really was no need for any type of food that wasn't French. For an added flourish, hang orange-peel strips over the edge of the punch bowl.

1⅔ cups (385 ml) aged rum

1⅔ cups (385 ml) brandy

¼ cup (60 g) sugar

Peel of 1 lemon, cut into strips

¼ teaspoon ground cinnamon, or ½ cinnamon stick

¼ teaspoon ground cloves, or 6 whole cloves

2¼ cups (560 ml) hot strong black tea

8 orange slices

Combine the rum, brandy, sugar, lemon peel, cinnamon, and cloves in a saucepan over medium-high heat and heat until just below boiling, stirring to dissolve the sugar. Pour the hot mixture into a heatproof punch bowl or other serving vessel. Add the hot tea and orange slices and stir briefly. Serve immediately in heatproof glasses, small mugs, or punch cups.

MAKES 6–8 COCKTAILS

BOURBON MAPLE FIZZ

This drink benefits from a large ice cube as opposed to crushed ice or standard ice cubes. The difference results in a chilled drink that isn't instantly watered down by melting ice.

2 oz (60 ml) bourbon

½ oz (15 ml) maple syrup

½ oz (15 ml) fresh orange juice

3 oz (90 ml) dark stout beer

3-inch (7.5-cm) strip orange peel

In a rocks glass, combine the bourbon, maple syrup, and orange juice. Place an ice cube in the glass and stir to chill the drink. Pour the dark stout over 1 large ice cube. Light a match to the orange peel, blow it out, and drop the peel into the glass.

MAKES 1 COCKTAIL

SPARKLING CORPSE REVIVER

This gin-based cocktail is one of the best-known members of the "corpse reviver" family of drinks that purportedly cure a hangover. A splash of club soda speeds the recovery.

¾ oz (20 ml) gin

¾ oz (20 ml) Lillet

½ oz (15 ml) Cointreau

½ oz (15 ml) fresh lemon juice

1 dash absinthe

1 oz (30 ml) club soda

1 Luxardo maraschino cherry

In a cocktail shaker filled with ice, combine the gin, Lillet, Cointreau, lemon juice, and absinthe. Cover, shake vigorously, and strain into a chilled coupe glass. Top with the club soda and garnish with the maraschino cherry.

MAKES 1 COCKTAIL

SCOTCH MANHATTAN

A twist on the classic Manhattan cocktail (page 160), the Scotch Manhattan is said to have originated in 1894 at New York's Waldorf-Astoria hotel. Its inspiration was the local premiere of an operetta about the life of Rob Roy MacGregor, known as the Scottish Robin Hood.

2 oz (60 ml) blended scotch whisky

1 oz (30 ml) sweet vermouth

2 dashes Angostura or other aromatic bitters

2 cherries, for garnish

Combine the whisky, vermouth, and bitters in a mixing glass filled with ice and stir until well chilled, 20–30 seconds. Strain into a chilled coupe or cocktail glass. Garnish with the cherries pieced together with a cocktail pick.

MAKES 1 COCKTAIL

POMME D'AMOUR

A riff on the classic version of the Sazerac, this drink mixes whiskey with French brandy. The name translates into "toffee apple," and the flavors are perfect for the fall

1 demerara sugar cube

2 dashes Peychaud's bitters

2 dashes apple bitters

1 oz (30 ml) rye whiskey

1 oz (30 ml) Calvados apple brandy

Absinthe, to rinse glass

Lemon twist, for garnish

Fill an old-fashioned or a rocks glass with ice and set aside. In a pint or mixing glass, add the sugar cube and soak it with the bitters, then muddle. Add the rye whiskey and Calvados and stir until the sugar dissolves. Add ice, then stir to chill the drink. Remove the ice from the old-fashioned glass, pour in the absinthe, and swirl to coat the glass. Strain the cocktail from the pint or mixing glass into the prepared old-fashioned glass. Flame the lemon twist over the drink and place swath in the drink.

MAKES 1 COCKTAIL

IN FULL FIG

Any variety of fig will do nicely here, but the type of fig will affect the flavor profile. Sweet figs will have more of a brown sugar flavor, while berry figs will provide a fruit note akin to strawberries.

2 figs, stemmed and halved

2 oz (60 ml) bourbon

1 oz (30 ml) lemon juice

½ oz (15 ml) honey

1 egg white

Dash angostura bitters

In a cocktail shaker, muddle the figs. Add the bourbon, lemon juice, honey, egg white, and bitters and shake for 1 minute. Add 1 cup ice and shake for another minute. Strain into a coupe glass.

MAKES 1 COCKTAIL

BLOOD ORANGE TEQUILA TROPI-CAL

You'll want a tequila that's been slightly aged for this drink—reposado is the natural choice, as the oak barrels that age the liquor soften the spirit's flavors just enough to smooth the agave flavor. Añejo tequila, aged one to three years, has a rounder, sweeter flavor, but you're better off treating it like a sipping drink than a mixer.

4 oz (125 grams) fresh
pineapple chunks

2 oz (60 ml) fresh blood orange juice

1½ oz (45 ml) tequila reposado

½ oz (15 ml) fresh lime juice

¼ oz (7 ml) Simple Syrup
(page 176)

1 oz (30 ml) club soda

Blood orange slice,
for garnish

In a cocktail shaker, muddle the pineapple and blood orange juice. Add the tequila, lime juice, simple syrup, and 1 cup of ice. Shake until chilled, about 30 seconds. Strain into an ice-filled rocks glass, top with club soda, and garnish with the blood orange slice.

MAKES 1 COCKTAIL

SMOKY PUMPKIN

Lapsang souchong, a black tea originating in China, is this cocktail's secret weapon. The raw leaves are smoke-dried over a pinewood fire, resulting in a woodsy, resinous flavor profile with just a slight pepperiness akin to smoked paprika.

¼ cup (60 ml) Winter Squash Purée (page 180)

3 oz (90 ml) Lapsang Souchong tea, at room temperature

1 oz (30 ml) maple syrup

6 tablespoons (90 ml) nonalcoholic apple cider or apple juice

Apple slice, for garnish (optional)

Combine all the ingredients in a cocktail shaker and shake until chilled. Strain into a rocks glass and garnish with an apple slice, if using.

MAKES 1 COCKTAIL

CARDAMOM APPLE PIE

If all you have on hand is apple juice, but you enjoy the comforting spices of apple cider, you can bolster the juice's flavor by adding a few ingredients to the pot. A cinnamon stick, whole nutmeg, whole allspice, and dried orange slices are a good base to start with, but you can play with any flavors you wish.

¾ cup (180 ml) nonalcoholic apple cider or apple juice

1½ teaspoons dried goji berries

¼ cup (60 ml) maple syrup

¼ oz (7 g) dried orange

4 whole cloves

2 cardamom pods

½ oz (15 g) dried apple, plus more for garnish

In a small pan, combine all the ingredients and simmer over medium-low heat for 10 minutes until hot. Once heated through and the flavors have infused, strain into a mug or heatproof glass. Garnish with a dried apple slice.

MAKES 1 COCKTAIL

PERSIMMON CINNAMON TEA

This tea provides a comforting, spicy boost perfect for those colder autumnal days. If you choose to spike this drink, opt for a whiskey that has tasting notes of vanilla, nuts, or fruits like orange and apple.

2 pieces dried persimmon

⅞ cup (7 oz) water

1–2 tablespoons brown sugar
(depending on how sweet
you want it to be)

½-inch (12-mm) piece of ginger

1½ oz (45 ml) whiskey (optional)

1 cinnamon stick,
for garnish

In a small pan, combine 1 piece dried persimmon with the remaining ingredients, except for the whiskey, if using, and the cinnamon stick, and bring to a boil. Reduce the heat, cover, and simmer for 10 minutes. Pour into a mug or heatproof glass, stir in whiskey, if using, and serve with remaining piece of dried persimmon and the cinnamon stick.

MAKES 1 COCKTAIL

SALTED CARAMEL COFFEE

This blend of salty-sweet caramel sauce and coffee with a touch of cocoa and rum is an indulgent after-dinner delight.

½ cup (125 ml) whole milk

2 tablespoons Salted Caramel (page 178), plus more for garnish

1 teaspoon unsweetened cocoa powder

¾ cup (180 ml) hot black coffee

2 tablespoons dark rum

Fresh Whipped Cream (page 179), for garnish

In a small saucepan, combine the milk, caramel sauce, and cocoa powder. Heat over low heat until warm, stirring well until the powder is dissolved. Add the coffee and rum and stir again. Pour into a coffee mug or cup, garnish with whipped cream, drizzle with additional caramel sauce.

MAKES 1 COCKTAIL

APPLE GINGER WHISKEY SOUR

A "dry shake" is a cocktail shaken without ice. Dry shaking is how certain cocktails get their airy, foamy texture, and it is essential to ensuring that an egg white is fully incorporated into the drink. After shaking, ice is added to the shaker, which is shaken again to chill the cocktail.

1 egg white	½ oz (15 ml) apple juice
½ oz (15 ml) fresh lemon juice	2 oz (60 ml) whiskey
½ oz (15 ml) ginger simple syrup (see note)	Lemon twist, for garnish (optional)
	Angostura bitters, for garnish

In a cocktail shaker, combine the egg white, lemon juice, simple syrup, apple juice and whiskey and dry-shake until foamy, about 10 seconds. Add a handful of ice to the shaker and shake until cold, about 10 seconds. Double-strain into a cold glass. Express lemon twist and top with bitters.

MAKES 1 COCKTAIL

LIBATION NOTE: To make the ginger syrup, combine 1-inch piece peeled fresh ginger, ½ cup cane sugar, and ½ cup water in a small sauce pan over low heat. Simmer for 15 minutes until fragrant, or longer for a more intense flavor.

BRANDIED MOCHA COFFEE

Brandy-laced, chocolate-flavored coffee always hits the spot. This is a delightful after-dinner drink.

½ cup (125 ml) whole milk

1 teaspoon unsweetened cocoa powder

1½ teaspoons sugar

2 teaspoons brandy

¾ cup (180 ml) hot black coffee

Fresh Whipped Cream (page 179) for garnish

In a medium saucepan, heat the milk over medium heat. Add the cocoa powder and sugar and stir until they are dissolved and the mixture is steaming but not boiling. Stir in the brandy. Slowly pour the hot coffee into the milk mixture, stirring constantly. Pour into a large coffee mug or cup and garnish with whipped cream.

MAKES 1 COCKTAIL

KIR ROYAL

This iconic French cocktail was named for a certain Canon Félix Kir, once mayor of Dijon, France, a city that produces crème de cassis from local black currants

5 oz (160 ml) Champagne or
sparkling wine, chilled

2 barspoons crème de cassis

Lemon twist, for garnish

Pour the Champagne and cassis into a chilled Champagne flute and stir briefly. Express the lemon twist over the drink and drop it into the glass

MAKES 1 COCKTAIL

LIBATION NOTE: Making a drink "royal" simply means adding sparkling wine to it. It works with any drink that could use a little lengthening or in which soda water is used.

SUNSET IN THE GARDEN

If you've never tried elderflower liqeur, you're about to find a new cocktail ingredient. Often known by its most common brand, St-Germain, it adds a vibrant floral taste that goes wonderfully with any sparkling wine. Here, mezcal and grapefruit juice are added to the mix, which really makes it shine.

1½ oz (45 ml) mezcal joven

¾ oz (23 ml) elderflower liqueur, preferably St-Germain

¼ oz (8 ml) fresh lime juice

¾ ounce (23 ml) fresh grapefruit juice

Sparkling white wine, such as cava, to top

Grapefruit twist, for garnish

In a cocktail shaker with ice, combine the mezcal, elderflower liqueur, lime juice, and grapefruit juice. Cover, shake vigorously until cold and well blended, and double-strain into a coupe glass or flute. Top with the sparkling wine. Garnish with the grapefruit twist.

MAKES 1 COCKTAIL

CHAI-SPICED HOT TODDY

Winter parties, or any cool-weather gathering, are an ideal occasion for batched hot toddies. Use a rail liquor here—the potent spices and citrusy notes will mask the taste of any low-quality rum. Vary the amount of honey for desired sweetness.

20 cardamom pods, gently crushed

10–12 cinnamon sticks, divided

10 whole cloves

3-inch (7.5 cm) piece of fresh ginger, unpeeled, thinly sliced

2 oranges, peeled into 3-inch (7.5-cm) strips, divided

8 cups (2 L) water

4 tablespoons (35 g) whole leaf black tea or tea bags

6 tablespoons (120 g) honey, or more or less as desired

Juice of 1 lemon

8 oz (250 ml) dark rum, whiskey or brandy

In a large pot over medium-high heat, toast the cardamom, 5 cinnamon sticks, and the cloves until fragrant, about 1 minute. Add the ginger, half of the orange peel strips, and the water, and raise the heat to high and bring to a boil.

Reduce the heat, cover, and simmer for 15 minutes to allow the flavors from the spices to brighten. Remove from the heat, add the tea, and allow to steep for 5 minutes. Strain the mixture through a fine-mesh sieve into another large pot and place over low heat, then stir in the honey, lemon juice, and the rum. Divide among mugs and garnish with a cinnamon stick and the remaining orange peels.

MAKES 4–6 COCKTAILS

MAMACITA
(MEZCAL SIDE CAR)

The beet gives this cocktail a rich, red color and thicker mouthfeel. The beet will cook through in about ten minutes, but since you'll be double-straining the contents of your drink, don't worry about overcooking them. Take caution when handling cooked beets—they'll stain skin and clothing.

Cane sugar for rimming glass

Lime wedge

5 fresh blackberries

½ oz (15 ml) fresh lime juice

1 small peeled and steamed beet, about 1½ oz (45 g), quartered

½ oz (15 ml) orange liqueur, such as curaçao or triple sec

1½ oz (45 ml) mezcal, or more to taste

On a small plate, spread an even layer of sugar. Gently rub the lime wedge around the rim of a small tumbler glass. Holding the base of the glass, dip the rim into the sugar. Set the glass aside.

In a cocktail shaker, muddle the blackberries and lime juice together. Add the beet, liqueur, mezcal, and a handful of ice. Cover, shake vigorously for 10 seconds, then double-strain into the prepared glass.

MAKES 1 COCKTAIL

LIBATION NOTE: This is a smaller cocktail than many. If you want to fill a larger glass, double the amounts of the lime juice, liqueur, and mezcal.

GOOD MORNING GREY

Made with Earl Grey tea, this cocktail's honey and caffeine make for a fantastic brunch option—especially for those guests nursing hangovers from the night before.

8 oz (2 L) water

1 bag Earl Grey tea

1 tablespoon honey

1 tablespoon fresh lemon juice

1 oz (30 ml) bourbon, or more to taste

Lemon slices, for garnish

Cinnamon stick, for garnish

Rosemary sprig, for garnish (optional)

In a small saucepan, bring the water to a boil. Add the tea and let steep for 5 minutes over low heat. Add the honey and lemon juice and stir until dissolved. Stir in the bourbon and pour into a mug. Garnish with lemon slices, a cinnamon stick, and a rosemary sprig, if using.

MAKES 1 COCKTAIL

MEZCAL SOUR

A sour is any cocktail that has a raw egg white in it. It might sound gross, but the egg white gives the drink a fuller mouth-feel and produces a delightful foam on the top. Add the bitters on top of the foam and use a toothpick to create designs for an extra-special presentation. If you don't want to use a raw egg white, you can substitute aquafaba, the juice from a can of chickpeas (garbanzo beans), for an almost identical effect.

2 oz (60 ml) mezcal joven

½ oz (15 ml) fresh lemon juice

¾ oz (20 ml) Simple Syrup (page 176)

1 egg white (pasteurized) or 1 oz (30 ml) aquafaba (chickpea juice)

2 dashes Amargo-Vallet bitters or Angostura aromatic bitters

In a cocktail shaker with ice, combine all the ingredients, except for the bitters. Cover and shake well for 30 seconds. Add ice and continue to shake until cold, 7–10 seconds more. Double-strain into a cocktail or coupe glass and add the bitters on top of the foam.

MAKES 1 COCKTAIL

WINTER

WILD MULE

This spicy, tangy drink saw an explosion of popularity in the 2010s, though it had been part of the cocktail lexicon for more than half a century. Legend has it that the drink was originally served in its signature copper mug to capture consumers' attention in order to sell bottles of Smirnoff vodka.

1 oz (30 ml) fresh lime juice

½ oz (15 ml) Simple Syrup (page 176)

Ginger beer, to top

Lime wedge, for garnish

2 thin jalapeño chile slices, for garnish

In a copper mug or an old-fashioned glass with ice, add the lime juice and simple syrup. Top with ginger beer and garnish with the lime wedge and jalapeño.

MAKES 1 COCKTAIL

BALTIMORE EGGNOG

This easy and delicious eggnog, which is basically a flip (see page 93) with milk, requires no cooking and shows up in almost every cocktail book of the mid-1800s in one form or another by the same name. Some versions of this recipe require only shaking, but this one, from Jerry Thomas's *The Bar-Tender's Guide*, calls for separating the egg, beating the white, and then mixing the white into the beaten egg yolk–spirit mixture for a frothy and delightful nog.

1 egg, separated

1½ barspoons Rich Simple Syrup (page 176)

1½ oz (45 ml) Cognac brandy or Jamaican rum or a mixture of both

1½ barspoons Madeira or port

½ cup (125 ml) whole milk

Ground or freshly grated nutmeg, for garnish

In a small bowl, using an electric mixer, beat the egg white until stiff peaks form. Set aside. In a separate small bowl, combine the egg yolk and simple syrup and beat until blended. Add the Cognac and Madeira and beat until blended. Add the milk and beat again. Finally, add the whipped egg white, beat just until combined, and transfer to a goblet or mug. Sprinkle with a little nutmeg.

MAKES 1 COCKTAIL

LIBATION NOTE: The foam created by beating the egg white is worth the effort, but if you're feeling lazy, just shake all the ingredients together in a cocktail shaker.

PERSIMMON NOG

The U.S. Food and Drug Administration generally discourages the consumption of raw eggs, but there are ways to minimize the risk of bacterial exposure. If you're concerned about consuming raw eggs, only buy pasteurized eggs, and make sure your eggnog is heated to 160°F before serving.

¾ cup (180 ml) milk

1 egg, whisked

¾ oz (20 ml) maple syrup

½ teaspoon ground cinnamon, plus more for garnish

¼ cup (55 g) Spiced Persimmon Purée (page 181)

In a small pan over low heat, warm the milk and add the egg slowly while whisking to make sure it doesn't cook in milk mixture. Heat until warm but not too hot, then remove from the heat. Add the remaining ingredients and stir to mix well. Garnish with a sprinkle of ground cinnamon on top.

MAKES 1 COCKTAIL

GINGERBREAD DARK & STORMY

Gingerbread simple syrup gives this seafarer's drink from Bermuda a more complex flavor, playing off the caramel overtones of the dark rum and the spicy kick of the ginger beer. Traditionalists use Bermuda's own Gosling's Black Seal rum.

2 oz (60 ml) dark rum	3 oz (90 ml) ginger beer
¾ oz (20 ml) fresh lime juice	1 cinnamon stick, for garnish
½ oz (15 ml) Gingerbread Simple Syrup (page 176)	1 slice crystallized ginger, for garnish

In a chilled highball glass, combine the rum, lime juice, and gingerbread syrup. Add ice and stir. Top with the ginger beer and more ice. Garnish with the cinnamon stick and crystallized ginger.

MAKES 1 COCKTAIL

NEW YORK SOUR

Essentially a wine-topped whiskey daisy—the daisy being a sour topped with seltzer—the New York sour is an elegant drink that would work well with hors d'oeuvres. Note that claret is an old British term for red wines from Bordeaux, but any nice fruity red wine will work here.

2 oz (60 ml) whiskey

¾ oz (20 ml) Simple Syrup (page 176)

¾ oz (20 ml) fresh lemon juice

About ¾ oz (20 ml) seltzer water

About 1 oz (30 ml) claret

In a cocktail shaker, add the whiskey, simple syrup, lemon juice, and ice. Cover, and shake vigorously for 8–10 seconds. Strain into a chilled cocktail glass, top with seltzer water, then float with the claret, poured carefully onto the back of a barspoon to create a red layer (see note).

MAKES 1 COCKTAIL

LIBATION NOTE: The trick to floating—or layering—a liquor, wine, or other ingredient on top of a drink is easier than it looks, and all you need is a barspoon. Place the barspoon on the surface of the drink so the convex side sticks up, like a little metal island, then slowly pour the liquid onto the spoon. Because the claret in this sour is less dense than the cocktail, it will float as a separate layer.

CLASSIC PALOMA

Choose a good blanco tequila—or a reposado if you prefer a richer flavor—for this refreshing tequila cocktail. For a fizzier drink, mix as directed, skipping the fresh grapefruit juice and club soda to top off the glass with grapefruit soda (look for Jarritos brand from Mexico).

1 tablespoon salt for rimming glass	2 oz (60 ml) tequila
1 tablespoon sugar for rimming glass	1 oz (30 ml) fresh lime juice
Lime wedge	½ oz (15 ml) Simple Syrup (page 176)
3 oz (90 ml) fresh grapefruit juice	Grapefruit twist, for garnish

On a small plate, combine the salt and sugar and spread in an even layer. Gently rub the lime wedge around the rim of a tall Collins glass. Holding the base of the glass, dip the rim into the salt mixture. Set the glass aside.

In a cocktail shaker filled with ice, combine the grapefruit juice, tequila, lime juice, and simple syrup and shake until chilled, about 30 seconds. Fill the prepared glass with ice, then pour in the paloma. Garnish with the grapefruit twist.

MAKES 1 COCKTAIL

STOUT SANGAREE

This is a hearty drink that's perfect for enjoying near the fireplace in a pub. It is part of the sangaree category of mixed drinks, whose members are all made with a base wine, spirit, or beer and a sweetening agent. In this version, ruby port adds sweetness and brightness to the mix. Sangarees (whose name is a variant of sangria) can be served over ice, neat, or straight up in a wine glass or beer glass.

1¼ cups (310 ml) Irish stout

3 oz (90 ml) ruby port

Ground or freshly grated nutmeg, for garnish

Pour the stout and port into a large wine glass. Sprinkle with the nutmeg.

MAKES 1 COCKTAIL

LIBATION NOTE: For a twist with a deeper, more complex flavor, replace the ruby port with tawny port, which is aged longer to oxidize slightly. But scale back the amount of stout to let the flavors of the port shine.

TOM & JERRY

During the cold season, this early nineteenth-century drink will warm you up. Although it is traditionally served from a Tom and Jerry bowl into Tom and Jerry cups, any bowl and mugs will work. Don't beat the egg whites here to stiff peaks—all you need to add to the batter is some volume. You don't need structure, like you would for a meringue.

12 eggs, separated

1½ cups (375 g) sugar

1 teaspoon baking soda

2 cups (500 ml) dark rum

2 cups (500 ml) brandy

2 quarts plus 1 cup (2.1 L) whole milk, scalded

Ground or freshly grated nutmeg, for garnish

In a large bowl, combine the egg yolks, 1¼ cups (315 g) of the sugar, and the baking soda and whisk until the mixture is thick and creamy. In a Tom and Jerry bowl or other large bowl, using an electric mixer on medium speed, beat the egg whites until frothy. Sprinkle in the remaining ¼ cup (60 g) sugar, raise the speed to medium-high, and beat until soft peaks form. Using a rubber spatula, fold the egg whites into the egg yolk mixture just until combined, forming a thick batter.

Whisking constantly, gradually add the rum and brandy to the batter. Divide the batter evenly among 24 Tom and Jerry cups or heatproof punch cups (each should hold about ¾ cup [180 ml]). Add about ⅓ cup (80 ml) hot milk to each cup (just pour it in, don't stir). Sprinkle the nutmeg over each serving.

MAKES 24 COCKTAILS

HOT BUTTERED RUM

This sweet, spice-laced, spiked beverage has its origin in colonial America, where New England distillers were turning molasses imported from Jamaica into rum as early as the 1650s. The steaming-hot mix of the strong local spirit and rich butter provided a welcome defense against the bitter-cold Northeast winter. Don't be tempted to stir the melted butter into the drink. It should float on top.

2 oz (60 ml) dark rum

½ oz (15 ml) Simple Syrup (page 176)

3 whole cloves

1 cinnamon stick, about 3 inches (7.5 cm) long

½–⅔ cup (120–160 ml) boiling water

1 barspoon (about 1 pat) unsalted butter (see note)

Ground or freshly grated nutmeg, for garnish

Pour the rum and simple syrup into a heatproof mug or an Irish coffee glass. Add the cloves and the cinnamon stick. Pour in the boiling water almost to fill the glass. Float the butter on top (so it will melt slowly), then sprinkle with the nutmeg.

MAKES 1 COCKTAIL

LIBATION NOTE: Salted butter works well here, too, adding just enough salinity to brighten up the rum and spices.

HOT BUTTERED YUM

It's up to you whether or not you'd like to add unsalted or salted butter to this concoction. Unsalted butter will result in a smooth, sweet drink. Salted butter will, of course, add a touch of salt that elevates the other flavors of the drink.

½ cup (4 oz) butter, at room temperature

¾ cup (185 g) brown sugar

¾ cup (185 g) granulated sugar

1 teaspoon ground cinnamon

¼ teaspoon ground cloves

¼ teaspoon ground nutmeg

1½ cups (255 g) vanilla (or gingersnap) ice cream, slightly softened

Boiling water

Cinnamon stick and star anise, for garnish

To make the batter, mix the butter, sugars, and spices thoroughly in a bowl. Stir in the ice cream and mix until well combined. Transfer the batter to a container with a tight-fitting lid and store in the freezer for up to 2 weeks. To serve the hot buttered yum, place a portion of the batter in a mug or heatproof glass, fill with boiling water, and stir. Garnish with a cinnamon stick and star anise.

MAKES 2 COCKTAILS

PINING AWAY

This drink's deep flavor profile comes not just from the woodsy pine needles but also from the dash of maple syrup, so don't be afraid to break out the organic, high-quality maple syrup for this one. Cashew milk is ideal here, but you can substitute almond milk if you'd like.

Handful of conifer needles (can be substituted with white pine, spruce, or Douglas fir needles)

1 cup (250 ml) cashew milk

½ oz (15 ml) maple syrup

Ground or freshly grated nutmeg, for garnish

In a small pan over medium-high heat, combine the conifer needles and cashew milk and simmer for 30 minutes, or until the flavors are infused. Let cool. Place the cooled liquid and maple syrup in a cocktail shaker with ice and shake until chilled. Strain into a rocks glass filled with fresh ice and garnish with the nutmeg.

MAKES 1 COCKTAIL

BRANDY LIFT

The Brandy Lift cocktail was inspired by a love for New York–style egg creams and a desire to combine Cognac and Benedictine with one of the cocktail syrups that Jennifer Colliau produces at Small Hand Foods. The recipe is unusual because cream and seltzer cocktails usually contain eggs; since this is not quite a flip, she came up with the old-timey (but very modern) name "lift."

1½ oz (45 ml) Cognac or good brandy

½ oz (15 ml) Small Hand Foods orgeat

½ oz (15 ml) Benedictine liqueur

½ oz (15 ml) heavy cream

Seltzer water, to top

In a cocktail shaker with ice, combine the brandy, orgeat, Benedictine, and heavy cream. Cover and shake vigorously for 8–10 seconds. Strain into a chilled Collins or highball glass with fresh ice. Use a barspoon to paddle the drink furiously back and forth while adding seltzer to the rim of the glass. Let sit a minute or two to firm up the head, then slowly drizzle in more seltzer to lift the head above the rim of the drink. Serve with a straw.

MAKES 1 COCKTAIL

BLACK VELVET

This unlikely but elegant mixture of stout and sparkling wine was developed at Brooks's Club in London in 1861, to mourn the death of Prince Albert, Queen Victoria's prince consort. It is meant to symbolize the black band worn during mourning.

6 oz (180 ml) Irish stout, chilled

6 oz (180 ml) Champagne or sparkling wine, chilled

Carefully pour the stout and Champagne into a chilled pint glass or large wine glass.

MAKES 1 COCKTAIL

LIBATION NOTE: Sweeter sparkling wines work best here. If you're using dry sparkling wine, like a brut, add up to ½ oz (15 ml) simple syrup (page 176) to the drink to help the flavors meld.

MULLED WINTER PUNCH

Make the most of the holiday season with this spiced punch. If you can't find dried blood orange, simply double the amount of dried orange.

3 whole cloves

¼ cup (60 ml) pomegranate juice

¾ cup (180 ml) blackcurrant juice

2 fresh blackberries

Cinnamon stick, for garnish

¼ oz (7 g) dried orange, for garnish

¼ oz (7 g) dried blood orange, for garnish

In a small pan, combine all the ingredients except for the cinnamon stick and dried orange slices and bring to a boil. Reduce the heat and simmer for 10–15 minutes. Strain into a mug or heatproof glass and garnish with the cinnamon stick and dried orange slices.

MAKES 1 COCKTAIL

CITRUS & SPICED MULLED WINE

Mulled wine is a classic staple for European Christmas markets and long, frosty nights. It's important that the mixture doesn't boil—much like tea, these flavors benefit from a light steep and may turn bitter if scorched on the stove.

12 whole cloves

2 whole nutmeg seeds, cracked into pieces with a hammer

2 bottles (750 ml each) dry red wine

½ cup (120 g) sugar

Peel of 2 oranges and 2 lemons, plus more twists for garnish

¾ cup fresh orange juice

¼ cup fresh lemon juice

2 cinnamon sticks

Tie the cloves and nutmeg pieces in a small square of cheesecloth or put them in a large metal tea ball.

In a large pot over medium-low heat, combine the wine, sugar, orange and lemon peels, orange and lemon juices, cinnamon sticks, and the clove-and-nutmeg bundle. Heat over medium-low heat until steam begins to rise from the pot and the mixture is hot, about 10 minutes. Do not let it boil. Remove the clove-and-nutmeg bundle. Keep the wine warm over very low heat until ready to serve.

Ladle the wine into cups or heatproof glasses, garnish with the citrus twist, and serve warm.

MAKES 8–10 COCKTAILS

COFFEE COCKTAIL

This recipe, which originally appeared in Alfred Suzanne's 1904 book *La Cuisine et pâtisserie anglaise et américaine*, is a great way to have your after-dinner drink and coffee at the same time. It also makes for a potent brunch drink—think of it as a creamy coffee julep.

2 oz (60 ml) brewed espresso, at room temperature

2 oz (60 ml) brandy

2 oz (60 ml) heavy cream

1½ barspoons Simple Syrup (page 176)

Ground or freshly grated nutmeg, for garnish

In a cocktail shaker, combine the espresso, brandy, cream, simple syrup, and about 6 barspoons crushed ice. Cover and shake vigorously for 8–10 seconds. Pour the mixture, ice and all, into a Collins glass and sprinkle with the nutmeg. Serve with a straw.

MAKES 1 COCKTAIL

ICE COFFEE MOCKTAIL

If you can't beat the cold, join it! A fruit-forward whiskey would be ideal if you're looking to spike this mocktail—though you may have to adjust the milk for taste.

2 oz (60 ml) fresh orange juice

½ cup (125 ml) cold brewed coffee

2 tablespoons Allspice
Simple Syrup (page 176)

1½ tablespoons milk

Orange slice,
for garnish

In a cocktail shaker with ice, combine all the ingredients except for the orange slice. Shake vigorously until the mixture becomes frothy. Pour the contents into a tall glass filled with fresh ice and garnish with the orange slice.

MAKES 1 COCKTAIL

WINTER SPICED HIBISCUS

If you like wintry spices like ginger and cinnamon but want a little oomph, this drink is for you. It takes those classic cold-weather flavors and adds a twist of zesty lime and the bright tang of hibiscus flowers—a perfect drink for those who savor winter and those looking ahead to spring.

3½ cups (875 ml) water

1 tablespoon allspice berries

4 thin slices of ginger

1 cinnamon stick

1 tablespoon hibiscus flowers, plus more for garnish

Lime slices, for garnish

In a small pan over medium-high heat, combine 1¾ cups (430 ml) of the water, the allspice berries, ginger, and cinnamon and bring to a boil. Remove from the heat and stir in the hibiscus flowers, then cover and let sit for 30 minutes. Strain and pour into a large pitcher, add ice and remaining water. Pour into tall glasses filled with fresh ice and garnish with the hibiscus flowers and lime slices.

MAKES 4 COCKTAILS

BOURBON & COFFEE COCKTAIL

This after-dinner drink is a smooth blend of bourbon, coffee liqueur, and orange bitters. In addition to the well-known Kahlúa, there are a number of other interesting coffee liqueurs on the market such as Luxardo Sambuca Cream from Italy, Patrón XO Cafe Coffee Liqueur from Mexico, and Heering Coffee Liqueur from Denmark.

3 tablespoons bourbon

1 tablespoon coffee liqueur

2 dashes of orange bitters

Orange twist, for garnish

Fill a mixing glass with ice. Add the bourbon, coffee liqueur, and bitters and stir until chilled. Strain into a chilled cocktail glass and garnish with the orange twist.

MAKES 1 COCKTAIL

HIGHLAND HOLIDAY COCKTAIL

This drink, with a hint of mellow smokiness, is a good one to sip on in front of the fire after a long holiday meal.

¼ cup (60 ml) scotch whisky

2 tablespoons fresh lemon juice

1 tablespoon plus
1 teaspoon maple syrup

1 dash of Pastis

Sparkling apple cider, to top

1 apple slice, for garnish

Fill a cocktail shaker with ice. Add the scotch, lemon juice, maple syrup, and Pastis. Shake well and strain into a highball glass filled with ice. Top off with the apple cider and garnish with the apple slice.

MAKES 1 COCKTAIL

CAFFÈ CORRETTO

Caffè corretto literally means "corrected coffee" in Italian, and it is often served as a hair-of-the-dog drink in Italy. It consists of a shot of espresso with a shot of liquor such as sweet grappa, brandy, or Sambuca. Caffè corretto is also ideal for serving after dinner. Bring a variety of liqueurs to the table and let your guests choose their own to add to espresso.

1 cup (250 ml) hot espresso

1 tablespoon grappa,
brandy, or Sambuca

1 teaspoon sugar

Lemon twist, for garnish

Pour the espresso into an espresso cup. Add the liqueur and the sugar and stir well. Garnish with the lemon twist.

MAKES 1 COCKTAIL

HOT CHOCOLATE & PEPPERMINT SCHNAPPS

Here's a great recipe for an easy and fun holiday dessert. The peppermint flavor really shines through in these festive cups of cheer.

2 cups (500 ml) whole milk

4 oz (130 g) semisweet chocolate, chopped

¼ cup (60 ml) peppermint schnapps

Fresh Whipped Cream (page 179), for garnish

2 peppermint sticks or candy canes, for garnish

In a medium saucepan over low heat, heat half of the milk. Add the chocolate, stirring constantly, until melted. Raise the heat to medium and whisk in the remaining milk. Do not allow the mixture to boil.

Pour the hot chocolate into two coffee mugs or cups and stir in the peppermint schnapps, dividing it equally between the mugs. Garnish with the whipped cream and peppermint sticks.

MAKES 2 DRINKS

TUMERIC, APPLE & GINGER CHAI

Because boiling ground spices generally makes beverage concoctions bitter, using fresh turmeric root is the key to capturing the earthy, peppery nuance behind its bitterness. Just like with ground turmeric, fresh turmeric root can stain your skin, nails, and clothes, so use it with caution.

1 chai tea bag

1 cup (250 ml) water

½ oz dried apple, plus more for garnish

1-inch (2.5-cm) piece of fresh turmeric root

1 tablespoon dried ginger

About 2 tablespoons (20 g) sugar (depending on how sweet you want it to be)

¼ cup (60 ml) milk

Cinnamon stick, for garnish

In a small pan, combine the tea bag, water, apples, turmeric, and ginger and bring to a boil. Reduce heat, cover, and simmer for 15 minutes. Remove the tea bag. Add the sugar and milk and whisk until the sugar dissolves. Strain into a mug or heatproof glass and garnish with the cinnamon stick and dried apple.

MAKES 1 COCKTAIL

VANILLA-CITRUS OLD-FASHIONED

The addition of vanilla heightens similar notes in the whiskey, and the extra dose of citrus gives this cocktail classic a brighter flavor.

1-inch (2.5-cm) piece vanilla bean, plus 1 vanilla bean for garnish

2-inch (5-cm) piece lemon peel

2-inch (5-cm) piece orange peel

¼ oz (7 ml) Vanilla Simple Syrup (page 176)

3 dashes orange bitters

2 oz (60 ml) bourbon

Squeeze of fresh orange juice (optional), to top

Orange twist, for garnish

In a rocks glass, muddle the vanilla bean, lemon peel, orange peel, simple syrup, and orange bitters. Add 1 large ice cube and the bourbon, and stir gently. Top with the orange juice, if using. Garnish with the vanilla bean and orange twist.

MAKES 1 COCKTAIL

MEXICAN HOT CHOCOLATE

Chile liqueur is definitely worth seeking out for this recipe. Made from ancho chiles steeped in a sugar cane spirit, chile liqueur adds a sweet and smoky flavor to all kinds of drinks, including homemade hot chocolate.

1½ cups (375 ml) whole milk

2 tablespoons unsweetened cocoa powder

2 oz (60 g) unsweetened chocolate, chopped

2 tablespoons (20 g) sugar

1 star anise pod

1 vanilla bean, split

Pinch of cayenne pepper

Pinch of salt

2 oz (60 ml) tequila (optional)

1 tablespoon ancho chile liqueur, such as Ancho Reyes (optional)

2 orange twists, for garnish

In a medium saucepan over low heat, combine the milk, cocoa powder, and chocolate, and stir until the chocolate melts. Add the sugar, star anise, vanilla bean, cayenne pepper, and salt. Simmer for 10 minutes. Strain the mixture into two coffee mugs or cups and stir in the tequila and chile liqueur, if using, dividing them equally between the mugs. Garnish with the orange twists.

MAKES 2 DRINKS

WARMING MILK

Maca root is made by drying the root and grinding Peruvian ginseng into a fine powder (also known as maca flour). It is known for balancing hormones, boosting mood and libido, and sustaining energy. Because of its ability to alter hormones, use it with caution.

8 oz (250 ml) of dairy-free milk, warmed

1-inch piece fresh peeled turmeric root

Slice of fresh peeled ginger, about ⅛ inch thick

Pinch freshly cracked black pepper

¼ teaspoon Ceylon cinnamon

½ teaspoon maca root powder (optional)

2 teaspoons honey

In a blender, combine all the ingredients and blend until smooth. Pour the contents into a mug.

MAKES 1 COCKTAIL

LIBATION NOTE: If you don't have a blender, combine all the ingredients in a small saucepan over low heat and bring to a simmer. Cover the pan, remove from the heat, and let the ingredients seep for 5–10 minutes.

APPLE HOT TODDY

Adapted from one of the oldest cocktail recipes, this version omits the mashing of the apple into the drink, drawing a majority of its apple flavor from the brandy instead. Feel free to mash the apple into the drink if you'd prefer. If you opt for tradition, keep the peel on, as it contains a good deal of the aroma and flavor of the fruit.

1½ tablespoons (15 g) sugar

Boiling water, as needed

2 oz (60 ml) Calvados
or other apple brandy

¼ baked apple

Ground or freshly grated nutmeg,
for garnish

In a large heatproof mug, combine the sugar and a small amount of boiling water and stir until the sugar is dissolved. Pour in the brandy and enough boiling water to fill the mug and stir well. Add the baked apple and sprinkle a little nutmeg on top.

MAKES 1 COCKTAIL

LIBATION NOTE: Use a baking apple—such as Granny Smith, Gravenstein, or Jonathan—with good acidity and with firm flesh that won't fall apart in the toddy, leaving you with a warming treat once you finish the drink.

APPLE-BOURBON HOT TODDY

Apple cider and bourbon are a smooth and delicious combination. This spicy cocktail, garnished with whipped cream, is a perfect way to welcome the autumn season.

1½ cups (375 ml) apple cider

1 tablespoon brown sugar

½ teaspoon ground nutmeg

1 vanilla bean, split

One 2-inch (5-cm) piece orange peel

2 oz (60 ml) bourbon

Fresh Whipped Cream (page 179), for garnish

In a medium saucepan over medium heat, combine the apple cider, brown sugar, nutmeg, vanilla bean, and orange peel and simmer for 10 minutes. Divide equally between two Irish coffee glasses or heatproof mugs and top each drink with the bourbon. Garnish with whipped cream.

MAKES 2 COCKTAILS

SPIKED PEPPERMINT BARK HOT CHOCOLATE

Using peppermint bark offers you a shortcut for making a wonderfully rich wintertime cocktail: It's made with unsweetened chocolate, white chocolate, and crushed peppermint candies, but the proportions make for a minty-chocolatey treat with just enough sweetness to not be cloying.

2 cups (500 ml) whole milk

12 oz (about 1½ sheets) (375 g) Williams Sonoma Peppermint Bark, chopped into pieces, plus more for garnish

⅛ teaspoon kosher salt

1 teaspoon vanilla extract or paste

2–2½ oz (60–75 ml) vodka, plus more to taste

Fresh Whipped Cream (page 179), for garnish

Cacao powder, for garnish

Flake salt, for garnish

In a medium saucepan over medium-low heat, combine the whole milk, peppermint bark, and salt. Heat, whisking occasionally, until thoroughly combined. Stir in the vanilla and vodka. Pour into 2 mugs and top with whipped cream, peppermint bark pieces, cacao powder, and flake salt.

MAKES 2 COCKTAILS

ANYDAY CLASSICS & TWISTS

DAIQUIRI

Named for an area near the Cuban city of Santiago de Cuba, the daiquiri became popular after the recipe was introduced in 1909 at the Army and Navy Club in Washington, D.C., by a junior medical officer, Lucius W. Johnson. Originally built in a Collins glass and stirred, the daiquiri evolved into a shaken drink, but there's nothing wrong with having it over ice if the weather demands it.

2 oz (60 ml) white rum
¾ oz (20 ml) fresh lime juice
¾ oz (20 ml) Simple Syrup (page 176)
Lime slice, for garnish

In a cocktail shaker, combine the rum, lime juice, and simple syrup. Add ice, cover, and shake vigorously for 8–10 seconds. Strain into a chilled coupe or cocktail glass. Garnish with the lime slice.

MAKES 1 COCKTAIL

LIBATION NOTE: The daiquiri belongs to the family of mixed drinks known as sours or sour cocktails. You'd think that a recipe that calls for only three ingredients would be boring, but swap out the rum for tequila and you have a margarita, or trade it out for gin and you have a gimlet!

RASPBERRY-PEACH FROZEN DAIQUIRI

Blend up a double batch of this warm-weather refresher for your next alfresco party. You can easily replace the rum with coconut water for a virgin daiquiri.

Crushed freeze-dried raspberries for rimming glasses
1 lime wedge
1½ cups (185 g) frozen raspberries
1 cup (185 g) frozen peaches
6 oz (180 ml) coconut rum
4 oz (120 ml) fresh lime juice
6 tablespoons (80 g) sugar, plus more to taste
4 fresh raspberries, for garnish
4 peach slices, for garnish

On a small plate, spread the crushed freeze-dried raspberries in an even layer. Gently rub the lime wedge around the rim of a wine glass or coupe glass. Holding the base of the glass, dip the rim into the crushed raspberries. Repeat with 3 more glasses. Refrigerate until ready to use.

In a blender, combine the frozen raspberries and peaches, 4-6 ice cubes, coconut rum, lime juice, and sugar and blend on high speed until thoroughly combined, about 45 seconds. Taste and add more sugar, if desired. Pour the contents of the blender into the chilled glasses. Garnish each daiquiri with a fresh raspberry and a peach slice.

MAKES 4 COCKTAILS

THAI DAIQUIRI

This twist on the Cuban classic drops the liquor and adds kaffir lime leaves to the mix, giving the cocktail a distinct citrusy note with floral undertones.

2 kaffir lime leaves, plus more for garnish

2 oz (60 ml) fresh lime juice

1 oz (30 ml) soda water

1 oz (30 ml) Kaffir Lime & Rosemary Oleo Saccharum (page 179)

In a pint glass, muddle the kaffir lime leaves. Add the remaining ingredients and ice. Gently stir together, then strain into a coupe glass. Garnish with a lime leaf.

MAKES 1 COCKTAIL

BLOODY MARY

Bartender Fernand Petiot reportedly created this classic in the 1920s at Harry's New York Bar in Paris, an American-style bar owned at the time by a former well-known American jockey, Tod Sloan. The recipe has changed greatly over the years, and everyone seems to have a favorite take on it, calling for an extra pinch of one seasoning or another. This recipe is basic but well balanced.

2 oz (60 ml) vodka

4 oz (120 ml) tomato juice

½ oz (15 ml) fresh lime juice

¼ barspoon black pepper

¼ barspoon ground cumin

Generous pinch of salt

2 dashes Worcestershire sauce

2 dashes hot sauce

Lime wedge, for garnish

Celery stalk, for garnish

In a cocktail shaker with ice, combine the vodka, tomato juice, lime juice, pepper, cumin, salt, Worcestershire sauce, and hot sauce. Cover and shake vigorously for 8–10 seconds. Pour the mixture, ice and all, into a pint glass. Garnish with the lime wedge and celery.

MAKES 1 COCKTAIL

LIBATION NOTE: You can make up a batch of Bloody Marys the night before you plan to serve them, mixing together everything but the lime juice and garnishes and skipping the ice. Refrigerate in a tightly capped container. The next day, add the lime juice and serve over ice. Feel free to be generous with the garnishes, which can turn this drink from hangover helper into a full meal.

BLOODY MARIA
WITH MEZCAL

BLOODY MARIA WITH MEZCAL

For a Sunday-morning pickup, this mezcal version of the classic Bloody Mary (page 157) does the trick. Use your favorite homemade Bloody Mary mix recipe, or just go for a store-bought mix.

Chile salt for rimming glass
Lemon wedge for rimming glass
1½ oz (45 ml) mezcal
2 oz (60 ml) Bloody Mary mix of your choice
Roasted jalapeños, for garnish
Roasted tomatoes, for garnish

On a small plate, spread an even layer of chile salt. Gently rub the lemon wedge along the rim of a chilled rocks glass. Holding the base of the glass, dip the rim into the salt. Set the glass aside.

In a cocktail shaker with ice, combine the mezcal and Bloody Mary mix. Cover and vigorously shake together until cold and well blended. Strain into a rocks glass over ice. Garnish with roasted jalapeño and tomatoes.

MAKES 1 COCKTAIL

OLD-FASHIONED

If there were a grande dame of cocktails, this would be it. The drink is an evolution of the sling, one of the earliest cocktails that simply combined spirits with water and sweetener. Adding bitters made it what we today know as an old fashioned. In the nineteenth century it was known as a bittered sling; the name old-fashioned came later, when the drink was, by that time, old-fashioned.

1 sugar cube
2 dashes bitters (usually Angostura)
2 oz (60 ml) whiskey
Lemon twist, for garnish

Put the sugar into an old fashioned or a rocks glass, then add the bitters and a couple dashes of water—just enough to moisten the sugar. Using a muddler, crush the sugar, dissolving it as much as possible. Add 1 large ice cube and the whiskey and give everything a stir with a barspoon. Express the lemon peel over the drink and drop it into the glass.

MAKES 1 COCKTAIL

LIBATION NOTE: This formula works with almost any unsweetened spirit and almost any sweetener, along with any bitters. It's the perfect prescription for experimenting to find what combinations you like best.

MANHATTAN

The origins of the Manhattan cocktail are disputed, but the drink was developed sometime in the 1860s. Originally made with rye whiskey, it is often also made with bourbon and Canadian whisky. During prohibition, Canadian whisky was the bootleg spirit of choice, a custom that continued long after the country went dry.

2 oz (60 ml) rye whiskey

1 oz (30 ml) Italian (sweet) vermouth

2 dashes Angostura bitters

Cherries, for garnish

Combine all the ingredients except for the cherries in an ice-filled mixing glass and stir for 20–30 seconds until well chilled. Strain the cocktail into a chilled coupe or cocktail glass. Garnish with cherries pieced together with a cocktail pick.

MAKES 1 COCKTAIL

HIBISCUS & TART CHERRY MANHATTAN

The classic trio of whiskey, vermouth, and aromatic bitters is a bar favorite, made modern here with the rich flavors of hibiscus and cherry. Rye whiskey is typically preferred, but any type will do.

2 oz (60 ml) whiskey

½ oz (15 ml) sweet vermouth

½ oz (15 ml) Hibiscus Simple Syrup (page 176)

2 dashes angostura bitters

1 cherry ice cube (page181)

In a mixing glass, combine the whiskey, sweet vermouth, hibiscus simple syrup, and bitters. Add regular ice and stir well until chilled. Place the cherry ice cube in a rocks glass and strain the contents of the mixing glass into the rocks glass.

MAKES 1 COCKTAIL

BRANDY ALEXANDER

This creamy cocktail—a blend of brandy, crème de cacao, and cream—is beloved by many and a perfect choice for an after-dinner drink.

2 oz (60 ml) brandy

2 tablespoons dark crème de cacao

2 tablespoons half-and-half

Generous pinch of ground or freshly grated nutmeg, for garnish

In a cocktail shaker filled halfway with ice, combine the brandy, crème de cacao, and half-and-half. Cover and shake well. Strain into a martini glass and garnish with the nutmeg.

MAKES 1 COCKTAIL

CLASSIC NEGRONI

The most widely told legend describing the birth of this cocktail is that Count Camillo Negroni, of Florence, Italy, asked his bartender to use gin in place of the seltzer water in his Americano. The equal parts of each ingredient make it a simple but effective masterpiece.

1½ oz (45 ml) gin
1½ oz (45 ml) sweet vermouth
1½ oz (45 ml) Campari
Orange slice, for garnish

In a rocks glass with ice, combine all ingredients except for the garnish. Stir to combine and garnish with the orange slice.

MAKES 1 COCKTAIL

NOT YOUR NEGRONI

Sanbitter is a nonalcoholic apertivo. Much like Campari or Aperol, Sanbitter provides a bitter citrusy note but ends with a smooth, sweet finish. This will be your key ingredient to creating a formidable nonalcoholic negroni.

1 oz (30 ml) fresh orange juice
1 oz (30 ml) white grape juice
4 oz (125 ml) Sanbitter
Orange twist, for garnish

In a mixing glass with ice, combine all the ingredients, except for the orange twist, and stir until chilled. Strain into a rocks glass with fresh ice and garnish with the orange twist.

MAKES 1 COCKTAIL

FROZEN ORANGE NEGRONI

A traditional Negroni is made with Campari, sweet vermouth, and gin and is garnished with an orange peel. This is a refreshing riff on the classic that's made with fresh orange juice, Simple Syrup, and crushed ice.

2 oz (60 ml) fresh orange juice
2 tablespoons Campari
2 tablespoons gin
2 tablespoons sweet vermouth
1½ tablespoons Simple Syrup (page 176)
1 orange slice, for garnish

Put the orange juice, Campari, gin, vermouth, simple syrup, and about 4 tablespoons (80 g) ice in a blender and blend until smooth. Add another 4 tablespoons (80 g) ice and blend again until very smooth. Pour into a rocks glass and garnish with the orange slice.

MAKES 1 COCKTAIL

OAXACAN NEGRONI

Traditionally made with gin, Negronis taste equally great (maybe even better) with mezcal.

1 oz (30 ml) mezcal joven
1 oz (30 ml) Campari
1 oz (30 ml) sweet vermouth
Orange twist, for garnish

Pour all the liquid ingredients over ice into a rocks glass and stir until cold and well blended. Garnish with the orange twist.

MAKES 1 COCKTAIL

TARRAGON NEGRONI

In this riff on the edgy, strong Italian aperitif, the traditional sweet vermouth has been swapped out in favor of Bordeaux-based Lillet. Bittersweet Peychaud's and anise-scented tarragon finish the already heady mix.

2 oz (60 ml) gin
1 oz (30 ml) Campari
1 oz (30 ml) Lillet Blanc
1 oz (30 ml) fresh lemon juice
¼ oz (7 ml) Tarragon Simple Syrup (page 176)
1 dash Peychaud's bitters
1 tarragon sprig, for garnish

In a cocktail shaker filled with ice, combine the gin, Campari, Lillet, lemon juice, tarragon simple syrup, and Peychaud's bitters. Cover, shake vigorously, and strain into a chilled rocks or coupe glass. Add ice if desired and garnish with the tarragon sprig.

MAKES 1 COCKTAIL

MARGARITA

Because of their tart and not-too-sweet flavor, margaritas are very food-friendly cocktails. They pair well with spicy dishes such as salsas, tacos, and empanadas.

Kosher salt for rimming glass
1 lime wedge
2 oz (60 ml) tequila
1 oz (30 ml) triple sec
¾ oz (20 ml) fresh lime juice
Lime slice, for garnish

On a small plate, spread salt in an even layer. Gently rub the lime wedge around the rim of a coupe glass. Holding the base of the glass, dip the rim into the salt. Set aside.

In a cocktail shaker filled with ice, combine the tequila, triple sec, and lime juice. Cover, shake well, and strain into the prepared glass. Garnish with a lime slice.

MAKES 1 COCKTAIL

MOJITO

While the exact origins of this cocktail are murky, we know it's of Cuban origin. Some legends say that Francis Drake developed a rudimentary version of the cocktail in the 16th century, while others claim that slaves working the Cuban sugarcane fields in the 19th century invented the drink. One thing everyone can agree on is that on a hot day there's nothing better.

15 fresh mint leaves
¾ oz (20 ml) fresh lime juice
¾ oz (20 ml) Simple Syrup (page 176)
2 oz (60 ml) light rum
1 oz (30 ml) club soda
Mint sprig and lime slice, for garnish

In a mixing glass, muddle the mint, lime, and simple syrup with enough force to extract the mint oils but not so much that you rip the leaves.

Fill the glass with ice, and then add the rum and soda. Stir to incorporate the flavors, and transfer to a Collins glass. Garnish with mint and lime.

MAKES 1 COCKTAIL

MOCK MOJITO

Because ginger beer and ginger ale are similar, swapping out one for the other won't make a huge difference, but the difference is worth noting. Whereas ginger beer is made by fermenting and brewing ginger with other ingredients, ginger ale is made by combining carbonated water and ginger syrup. Ginger ale will you give you a more mellow, sweeter drink; ginger beer will make it zingy and spicy.

10 fresh mint leaves, plus sprigs for garnish
1 oz (30 ml) Simple Syrup (page 176)
1 oz (30 ml) fresh lime juice
7 oz (210 ml) ginger ale
Lime slice, for garnish

Muddle the mint leaves in a cocktail shaker, and add the syrup, lime juice, and ice. Cover and shake. Top with ginger ale, then strain into a rocks glass filled with fresh ice. Garnish with a mint sprig and lime slice.

MAKES 1 COCKTAIL

ROSEMARY-GINGER MOJITO

ROSEMARY-GINGER MOJITO

This modern take on the Cuban national cocktail adds ginger and rosemary to the classic minty mix— a fragrant and flavorful partnership that pairs perfectly with the vanilla tones of the rum. To release more flavor from the rosemary sprig, lightly bruise it before slipping it into the glass.

2 oz (60 g) crystallized ginger for rimming glass

½ cup (100 g) sugar for rimming glass

1 lime wedge

10 fresh mint leaves

2 oz (60 ml) white rum

1 oz (30 ml) fresh lime juice

½ oz (15 ml) Rosemary-Ginger Simple Syrup (page 176)

1 oz (30 ml) club soda

1 mint sprig, for garnish

1 rosemary sprig, for garnish

In a mini food processor, combine the crystallized ginger and sugar and pulse until finely ground. Pour the ginger-sugar mixture onto a small plate and spread in an even layer. Gently rub the lime wedge around the rim of a highball glass. Holding the base of the glass, dip the rim into the ginger-sugar mixture. Refrigerate until ready to use. Just before serving, fill the glass with ice.

In a cocktail shaker, muddle the mint leaves. Add the rum, lime juice, rosemary-ginger simple syrup, and ice.

Cover, shake vigorously, and strain into the ice-filled glass. Top with the club soda and garnish with the mint and rosemary sprigs.

MAKES 1 COCKTAIL

GIMLET

Some bartenders say that the proper way to make a gimlet is with lime cordial (like Rose's lime juice) and that making this drink with fresh lime juice is technically a Rickey. Lime juice advocates say that the drink with lime juice is the way the drink was intended to be made. If you want to find out for yourself, simply replace both the simple syrup and lime juice with ¾ ounce (20 ml) of lime cordial.

2 oz (60 ml) gin

½ oz (15 ml) fresh lime juice

½ oz (15 ml) Simple Syrup (page 176)

Lime slice, for garnish

In a cocktail shaker, combine all the ingredients except for the garnish. Add ice, cover, and shake well. Strain into a cold coupe or cocktail glass. Garnish with the lime slice.

MAKES 1 COCKTAIL

CUCUMBER-BASIL GIMLET

Traditionally, a gimlet is comprised mostly of two parts: either gin or vodka, and sweetened lime juice. Lime slices or pickled mushrooms or onions garnish the drink. Here, a simple garnish of cucumber or light-flavored fruits like honeydew or cantaloupe would make for an excellent pairing.

6 fresh basil leaves, plus more for garnish
4 cucumber slices, plus more for garnish
1½ oz (45 ml) fresh lime juice
1½ oz (45 ml) Simple Syrup (page 176)
2 oz (60 ml) water

In a cocktail shaker, muddle the basil leaves and cucumber. Add the lime juice, simple syrup, water, and ice and shake until chilled. Strain into a rocks glass filled with fresh ice and garnish with the remaining basil and cucumber.

MAKES 1 COCKTAIL

GRAPEFRUIT & SAGE GIMLET

In this gimlet redux, tangy grapefruit juice replaces the traditional lemon juice, and sage is added to impart an herbaceous flavor.

2½ oz (70 ml) gin

1 oz (30 ml) fresh grapefruit juice
½ oz (15 ml) Sage Simple Syrup (page 176)
1 grapefruit slice, for garnish
1 fresh sage leaf, for garnish

In a cocktail shaker filled with ice, combine the gin, grapefruit juice, and sage simple syrup. Cover, shake vigorously, and strain into an ice-filled rocks glass. Garnish with the grapefruit slice and sage leaf.

MAKES 1 COCKTAIL

COSMOPOLITAN

The origins of the ubiquitous "cosmo" are, like many things that occur in bars, hazy. Some claim the drink was invented in the 1970s in Cleveland—or South Beach or Minneapolis—as a variation of a kamikaze (a cosmopolitan without the cranberry juice). It's also entirely possible the origins of the drink come from the 1934 book *Pioneers of Mixing at Elite Bars*, which includes a recipe utilizing gin instead of vodka and Raspberry Simple Syrup (page 176) in place of the cranberry juice.

2 oz (60 ml) vodka
¾ oz (20 ml) fresh lime juice
¼ oz (7 ml) cranberry juice
½ oz (15 ml) orange liqueur or triple sec
Lime slice, for garnish

In a cocktail shaker, combine all the ingredients except for the garnish. Add ice, cover, and shake vigorously for 8–10 seconds. Strain into a cold coupe or cocktail glass. Garnish with the lime slice.

MAKES 1 COCKTAIL

BLOOD ORANGE COSMOPOLITAN

A staple of girlfriend get-togethers and parties of all kinds, the cosmopolitan sheds its signature deep red cranberry juice in favor of the aromatic, scarlet juice of the blood orange in this updated version of the festive classic.

2 oz (60 ml) vodka

1 oz (30 ml) Cointreau

1 oz (30 ml) fresh blood orange juice

½ oz (15 ml) fresh lime juice

½ oz (15 ml) Simple Syrup (page 176)

Blood orange slice, for garnish

In a cocktail shaker filled with ice, combine the vodka, Cointreau, blood orange juice, lime juice, and simple syrup. Cover, shake vigorously, and strain into a chilled martini glass. Garnish with the blood orange slice floated on top.

MAKES 1 COCKTAIL

SANGRIA

Occasionally, you won't want to make a big batch of sangria just to get a glass or two to enjoy in the garden on an unexpectedly chore-free afternoon. The key to this drink is the fruit garnish, so use whatever you have handy: sliced citrus, strawberries, peaches, apples—anything ripe and in season. Without the fruit, it's just a wine cocktail.

3 oz (90 ml) cheap and cheerful red wine

1½ oz (45 ml) orange liqueur, or ½ oz (15 ml) Rich Simple Syrup for a less boozy option (page 176)

½ oz (15 ml) fruit liqueur (berry liqueurs work well)

½ oz (15 ml) fresh lemon juice

1 oz (30 ml) fresh orange juice (other juices work well too)

1 oz (30 ml) soda water

Sliced fruit, for garnish

In a cocktail shaker with ice, combine the red wine, orange liqueur, fruit liqueur, and the lemon and orange juices. Cover and shake vigorously for 8–10 seconds. Strain into a Collins or highball glass with fresh ice. Top with the soda water and stir in gently. Garnish with fruit slices.

MAKES 1 COCKTAIL

MOCK SANGRIA

Fresh and fruity, this summery sangria is the perfect opportunity to take advantage of all the fresh fruits available at farmers' markets. You'll want to refrigerate the drink for thirty minutes not only to chill the mixture, but also to allow the fruit flavors to meld together.

16 oz (500 ml) acai juice
4 oz (125 ml) fresh orange juice
4 oz (125 ml) white grape juice
¼ lb (30 g) sliced strawberries
½ apple, diced
1 small orange, sliced
1 cup (250 ml) soda water

Combine all the ingredients, except for the soda water, in a large pitcher. Chill in the refrigerator for 30 minutes. When ready to serve, add the soda water and pour into wine glasses filled with ice.

MAKES 6–8 COCKTAILS

ROSÉ & PEACH SANGRIA

Sangria is not always made with red wine and brandy. Here is a light and lovely version made with rosé, vodka, and fresh peaches.

1 bottle (750 ml) rosé
¾ cup (180 ml) vodka
½ cup (125 ml) peach nectar
2 tablespoons (20 g) sugar
1 lb (500 g) ripe peaches, pitted and thinly sliced
1 cup (125 g) fresh raspberries
1–2 cups (250–500 ml) club soda

Pour the rosé, vodka, and peach nectar into a pitcher. Add the sugar and stir until dissolved. Add the peaches and raspberries and stir. Cover and refrigerate for 4 hours or until ready to serve.

Before serving, top off the sangria with club soda. Pour the sangria over ice in tall glasses.

MAKES 6–8 COCKTAILS

MICHELADA

The Michelada may sound like nothing more than the beer version of a Bloody Mary, but this cocktail varies widely—from a simple combination of lime, salt, and beer to more complicated brunch affairs. For a lighter morning cocktail with less acidity, this Michelada will do the trick.

Salt or Tajín (a Mexican chile-and-citrus salt blend) for rimming glass

1 lime wedge

3 oz (90 ml) tomato juice (or Clamato)

2 oz (60 ml) fresh lime juice

4 dashes Maggi seasoning sauce (or soy sauce)

3 dashes hot sauce (bottled Mexican, Tabasco, or Crystal—or even sriracha—work here), or more if you like the heat

1 pinch salt

12-oz can (355 ml) Mexican beer or lager, ice cold

On a small plate, spread a thin layer of salt (or Tajin). Gently rub the lime wedge around the rim of a pint glass. Holding the base of the glass, dip the rim into the salt.

Add ice to the glass, then the tomato juice, lime juice, Maggi, hot sauce, and salt. Stir, then add as much beer as will fit in the glass and still leave a few fingers of space at the top.

MAKES 1 COCKTAIL

IRISH COFFEE

An easy-drinking hot cup of coffee sweetened with a little sugar and braced with a shot of Irish whiskey, the Irish Coffee is an ageless classic. Originally created by a County Limerick chef for weather-weary travelers in the 1940s, the drink has spread around the world.

FOR THE CREAM:

2 oz (60 ml) heavy cream

1½ teaspoons sugar

1½ oz (45 ml) Irish whiskey

3 oz (90 ml) coffee

2 teaspoons sugar

In a chilled cocktail shaker, combine the heavy cream and 1½ teaspoons sugar. Cover and shake until the cream thickens and the sugar dissolves. You don't need stiff peaks—nor butter (which will happen if you shake too long). Set aside.

Combine the remaining ingredients in an Irish coffee glass and stir to combine. Top with a float of cream.

MAKES 1 COCKTAIL

SALTED CARAMEL IRISH COFFEE

One of the best antidotes to a winter's day, Irish Coffee takes on a rich, caramel sweetness in this updated version of the Gaelic favorite.

1 cup (250 ml) freshly brewed hot coffee

2 oz (60 ml) Baileys Irish Cream

2 tablespoons Salted Caramel (page 178), plus more for serving

Fresh Whipped Cream (page 179), for garnish

Flaky sea salt, for sprinkling

In a large mug, combine the coffee, Baileys Irish Cream, and salted caramel and stir until the caramel is completely melted. Top with whipped cream, drizzle with the salted caramel, and sprinkle with sea salt

MAKES 1 COCKTAIL

PIÑA COLADA

At the risk of quoting the popular Jimmy Buffet song, this summertime drink invites you to escape with its tropical flavors of pineapple and coconut. Spiking this cocktail is as easy as dropping in a shot of light rum and giving the drink a quick stir.

3 oz (90 ml) pineapple juice

4 oz (125 ml) cream of coconut

Pineapple wedge, maraschino cherry, and mint sprig, for garnish

Combine the pineapple juice, ⅔ cup (95 g) crushed ice, and cream of coconut in a blender and blend until smooth. Pour into a tall glass and garnish with a pineapple wedge, cherry, and mint.

MAKES 1 COCKTAIL

BLACK RUSSIAN

A Black Russian is a thoroughly satisfying drink to sip slowly. It's simple to make since it requires nothing more than shots of vodka and coffee liqueur poured over ice. A marinated cherry is an excellent garnish.

2 oz (60 ml) vodka

3 tablespoons coffee liqueur

1 marinated cherry, for garnish

Fill a rocks glass with ice. Add the vodka and coffee liqueur, swirl, and garnish with the cherry.

MAKES 1 COCKTAIL

WHITE RUSSIAN

Here is another easy and delightful drink made with vodka, coffee liqueur, and a splash of half-and-half. Black and White Russians have no Russian roots; they are named so simply because they are made with vodka.

2 oz (60 ml) vodka

3 tablespoons coffee liqueur

3 tablespoons half-and-half

Fill a rocks glass with ice. Add the vodka and coffee liqueur. Drizzle in the half-and-half.

MAKES 1 COCKTAIL

PEPPERMINT WHITE RUSSIAN

Peppermint on the rim and in the glass gives this old favorite a new flavor. Here, the half-and-half is stirred in, but some White Russian drinkers insist that it be floated on top. If you don't want to fuss with the cream, omit it and you'll have a Black Russian.

Half-and-half for rimming glass

1½ oz (45 ml) crushed peppermint candies for rimming glass

1½ oz (45 ml) Kahlúa

1 oz (30 ml) vodka

1 oz (30 ml) peppermint schnapps

Pour some half-and-half into a small, shallow bowl. On a small plate, spread the peppermint candies in an even layer. Holding the base of a rocks glass, dip the rim into the half-and-half and then into the candies. Place the glass in the refrigerator until ready to use.

Just before serving, fill the glass with ice. Add the Kahlúa, vodka, and peppermint schnapps and stir to combine. Add the 1½ oz (45 ml) half-and-half and stir until blended.

MAKES 1 COCKTAIL

DRY MARTINI

Popular in the 1920s, the dry martini differentiates itself from other martinis by using dry vermouth. A wet martini, by contrast, will be slightly sweeter as it uses more vermouth.

3 oz (90 ml) gin

½ oz (15 ml) dry vermouth

1 martini olive

In a cocktail shaker filled with ice, combine the gin and vermouth. Cover, shake vigorously, and strain into a chilled martini glass. Garnish with the olive.

MAKES 1 COCKTAIL

DIRTY MARTINI

There are many versions of the classic martini. Shaking the cocktail gives the cocktail body and texture as the ice shards emulsify.

If you're using stuffed blue cheese olives, use regular olive brine here instead of the blue cheese brine so the cocktail doesn't get too cloudy. For guests who are not keen on vermouth, rinse the glass with vermouth instead of shaking it with the other ingredients; shake the vodka and olive juice together and pour into the glass.

3½ oz (105 ml) vodka (the smoother the better)

1 oz (30 ml) green olive juice brine

¼ oz (7 ml) dry vermouth

Pitted green olive or stuffed blue cheese olive, for garnish

In a cocktail shaker with ice, combine the vodka, olive juice, and vermouth. Cover and shake vigorously for 10 seconds. Pour into a coupe class and garnish with the olive.

MAKES 1 COCKTAIL

FILIPPED MARTINI

By flipping the proportions of the standard two-to-one gin to vermouth ratio, you create a lighter drink that's more vermouth-heavy.

3¾ oz (110 ml) dry vermouth

¾ oz (20 ml) London Dry gin

Lemon twist, for garnish

Combine all the ingredients except for the lemon twist in a pint or mixing glass. Add ice and stir for 20–30 seconds until the temperature of the drink reaches 32°F (0°C). Strain the cocktail into a coupe or cocktail glass. Express lemon twist over the drink and drop it into the glass.

MAKES 1 COCKTAIL

RAMOS GIN FIZZ

Although this is the most famous fizz, it is actually not a true fizz because it departs from both the classic ingredients and method. The secret of this drink, created in the late nineteenth century by New Orleans restaurateur Henry Ramos, lies in the shaking: a full three minutes. That's a long time, but some feel it is the only way to achieve the cocktail's trademark silky mouthfeel. Feel free to shake it as long as you can.

2 oz (60 ml) gin
½ oz (15 ml) fresh lime juice
½ oz (15 ml) fresh lemon juice
½ oz (15 ml) Simple Syrup (page 176)
4 drops orange flower water
1 egg white
1 oz (30 ml) light cream (see note)
2 oz (60 ml) club soda

In a cocktail shaker, combine the gin, citrus juices, simple syrup, orange flower water, egg white, and cream. Add ice, cover, and shake vigorously for 3 minutes—or for as long as you can. Strain into a chilled wine glass or Collins glass. Add the club soda and stir briefly.

MAKES 1 COCKTAIL

LIBATION NOTE: Half-and-half or a mixture of equal parts whole milk and heavy cream works well if you cannot find light cream. If you double strain the drink by pouring it through a tea strainer or small fine-mesh sieve on its way into the glass, you will get finer bubbles and better texture in the drink.

METROPOLE

The Hotel Metropole, which once stood at the corner of Forty-second and Broadway in New York City, was well known for its eccentric clientele of bookies and cabaret performers. Essentially a nineteenth-century Cognac martini, the dry, almost-saline Metropole house cocktail is an elegant way to enjoy an old book.

1½ oz (45 ml) Cognac
1½ oz (45 ml) dry vermouth
2 dashes Creole bitters, such as Peychaud's
Dash orange bitters
2 cherries, for garnish

In a mixing glass filled with ice, combine the Cognac, vermouth, and both bitters and stir until well chilled, 20–30 seconds. Strain into a chilled cocktail glass or coupe. Garnish with the cherries pieced together with a cocktail pick.

MAKES 1 COCKTAIL

LIBATION NOTE: Swap out the dry vermouth for sweet vermouth and you have a bracing brandy drink for winter nights.

GRASSHOPPER

This classic after-dinner drink is made with crème de menthe, crème de cacao, and cream and is named for its color.

1 tablespoon plus 1 teaspoon crème de menthe

1 tablespoon plus 1 teaspoon white crème de cacao

2 teaspoons heavy cream

In a cocktail shaker with ice, combine the crème de menthe, crème de cacao, and cream. Cover and shake vigorously. Strain into a chilled cocktail glass.

MAKES 1 COCKTAIL

BASICS

SIMPLE SYRUP

MAKES ABOUT 1½ CUPS (375 ML)

1 cup (250 ml) water
1 cup (200 g) sugar
Infuser (see options below)

In a small saucepan over medium-high heat, bring the water to a simmer. Add the sugar and infuser of choice, if using, and stir until the sugar is dissolved. Remove from the heat and let cool. Strain the syrup through a fine-mesh sieve into a clean container, cover, and refrigerate for up to 2 weeks.

INFUSER OPTIONS

Allspice: 4 tablespoons crushed allspice

Basil: 15 fresh basil leaves, roughly chopped

Cinnamon: 2 cinnamon sticks

Gingerbread: 10 whole cloves, 2 cinnamon sticks, 2-inch (5-cm) piece peeled fresh ginger, 1 teaspoon ground cinnamon, 1 teaspoon ground ginger

Hibiscus: ½ cup (15 g) dried hibiscus flowers

Lemongrass: 1 lemongrass stalk, thinly sliced

Raspberry: 2 cups fresh raspberries

Rich Simple Syrup: Use a 2:1 ratio of sugar to water

Rosemary-Ginger: 2 tablespoons each chopped fresh rosemary and peeled fresh ginger

Sage: 10 fresh sage leaves, roughly chopped

Tarragon: 5 tarragon sprigs

Thyme: 10 thyme sprigs

Vanilla: 2 vanilla beans, split and seeds scraped

PEACH-BASIL SYRUP

MAKES ABOUT 1 CUP (240 ML)

1 cup (150 g) peaches, pitted and cut into wedges
1 cup (200 g) sugar
1 tablespoon fresh lemon juice
¼ cup (7 g) fresh basil leaves

In a saucepan over medium-high heat, combine the peaches, sugar, lemon juice, and basil and bring to a simmer. Reduce the heat to medium-low and continue to simmer, stirring frequently, until the peaches have broken down and become juicy, about 20 minutes. Strain the syrup through a fine-mesh sieve into a clean container, cover, and refrigerate for up to 5 days.

VARIATION: BLACKBERRY-THYME SYRUP
Replace the peaches with 1 cup (115 g) blackberries and the basil leaves with 2 fresh thyme sprigs.

RHUBARB SYRUP

MAKES ABOUT 6 OZ (180 ML)

1½ **cups diced fresh rhubarb**

Juice of 3 lemons

½ **cup (100 g) cane sugar**

1 vanilla bean, split, or 1 teaspoon vanilla bean paste

In a medium saucepan over medium-low heat, combine the rhubarb, lemon juice, sugar, and vanilla bean. Bring to a simmer, cover, reduce the heat, and simmer for 10 minutes. Stir the mixture, remove from the heat, and let steep for 10 minutes. Strain the mixture through a fine-mesh sieve into a bowl, then transfer to a jar until needed. The syrup will keep for 7 days.

SALTED CARAMEL

MAKES ABOUT 1 CUP (250 ML)

1 cup (200 g) sugar

6 tablespoons (80 g) unsalted butter, cut into 1-inch (2.5-cm) pieces, at room temperature

½ **cup (125 ml) heavy cream**

1½ **teaspoons kosher salt**

In a saucepan over medium-low heat, heat the sugar, stirring occasionally, until the sugar is melted and golden brown, about 7 minutes. Add the butter, one piece at a time, and stir until melted. Slowly stir in in the cream; the mixture will begin to bubble. Cook, stirring occasionally, until the cream is incorporated and the caramel begins to thicken, about 10 minutes.

Raise the heat to medium and cook, stirring occasionally, until the caramel is thickened and shiny, about 3 minutes. Add the salt and cook for 1 minute longer. Transfer the caramel to a heatproof container and let cool. Use at once, or cover and refrigerate for up to 1 week.

FRUIT SHRUBS

A shrub is made with fresh fruit, sugar, and vinegar, and it's a wonderful, refreshing beverage either on its own or added to a drink. Fill a tall glass with ice, add a splash of your preferred shrub and a shot of whiskey, gin, or vodka and you will have a lovely summer cocktail. It's also nice to add Champagne or sparkling wine to a fruit shrub.

MAKES ABOUT 3 CUPS

1 pound (500 g) chopped fruit

2 cups (500 g) sugar

2 cups (500 ml) white wine vinegar

Put the fruit in a large nonreactive bowl. Using a muddler or the back of a spoon, mash the fruit a bit. Add the sugar and toss well to combine. Cover the mixture with plastic wrap and let it sit in the refrigerator for 2 days, stirring occasionally.

Strain the mixture through a fine-mesh sieve, pressing on the solids to extract as much liquid as possible. Pour the liquid (shrub) into a clean, dry container with a lid. Add the vinegar and shake vigorously to combine. Put the shrub in the refrigerator for 5 days or up to a week, shaking the jar occasionally. The shrub will keep in the refrigerator for a few weeks. It should never be allowed to ferment or bubble. If it does, discard it.

LIBATION NOTE: Fruits that work well for shrubs include strawberries, raspberries, blueberries, blackberries, cherries, peaches, plums, and pears. Rhubarb, while technically a vegetable, is often eaten as a fruit and is also an excellent shrub ingredient. When preparing a shrub, use very ripe fruit. It should be thoroughly rinsed and may be peeled and chopped.

FRESH WHIPPED CREAM

MAKES ABOUT 2 CUPS

1 cup (250 ml) heavy cream, chilled

2 tablespoons (20 g) sugar

1 teaspoon vanilla extract

In a medium bowl with an electric mixer on high speed, whip the cream, sugar, and vanilla just until stiff peaks begin to form. If not using right away, cover with plastic wrap and refrigerate until ready to serve, up to 1 day. If the cream separates, whisk it again to its proper consistency before serving.

KAFFIR LIME & ROSEMARY OLEO SACCHARUM

MAKES 7 OZ (210 ML)

1 cup (220 g) superfine sugar

Zest of 8 kaffir limes

Leaves of 4 rosemary sprigs, chopped

2 oz (60 ml) hot water

Combine the sugar, zest, and rosemary in a bowl and massage together. Place the mixture in a resealable plastic bag and let rest for 1 hour. Add the hot water to dissolve any remaining sugar. Strain through a fine-mesh sieve into a clean container. The mixture can be stored in an airtight container in the refrigerator for up to 2 weeks.

TRIPLE ORANGE TINCTURE

MAKES ABOUT 5 OZ (160 ML)

3 oranges, organic and unwaxed if available

5 oz (160 ml) 151-proof vodka, or 2½ oz (75 ml) *each* Everclear and standard 80-proof vodka

Peel one of the oranges with a vegetable peeler to remove as much zest as you can with as little pith as possible. Place the peels on a parchment-lined baking sheet and dry at the lowest temperature in your oven until stiff, about an hour or two. Break the dried peels apart and place in a small mason jar.

Slice one orange in half. Peel one of the halves and add the peels to the mason jar. (Set the slices from this half aside for another use.) Cut and chop the other half (peel, flesh, and all) and add to the mason jar.

Peel the zest off half of the remaining orange and bake them on a parchment-lined baking sheet and dry at the lowest temperature in your oven until dried out, about an hour, then broil until the edges are burned. Keep a close eye on the peels, as they will burn very fast. Remove from the oven and let cool.

Tear or chop the burned peels and add them to the mason jar. Add the vodka to cover. Place in a cool, dark location, giving the jar a daily shake for three weeks. Then strain the solids and reserve the liquid.

CINNAMON-APPLE SYRUP

MAKES ABOUT 1 CUP (250 ML)

¾ cup (180 ml) apple cider

¼ cup (45 ml) honey

½ teaspoon ground cinnamon

In a small saucepan over medium-high heat, combine the apple cider and honey and bring to a simmer. Add the cinnamon and stir until dissolved. Remove from the heat and let cool. Pour the syrup into a clean storage container. Use at once, or cover and refrigerate for up to 2 weeks.

FRESH LEMONADE

Hot summer days call for refreshing lemonade served in tall glasses over ice. This recipe, made with freshly squeezed lemons and Simple Syrup, is a snap to make and can be used as a base for a number of summery drinks.

MAKES ABOUT 1½ QUARTS (1.5 L)

5 to 6 lemons

4 cups (1 L) cold water

¾ cup (180 ml) Simple Syrup (page 176)

Squeeze the lemons to make 1 cup of fresh lemon juice. Transfer to a large container or pitcher. Add the water and syrup and stir well. Refrigerate the lemonade for at least 1 hour before serving.

WINTER SQUASH PURÉE

MAKES ABOUT 2 CUPS, DEPENDING ON THE SIZE OF THE SQUASH

1 winter squash (such as butternut, pumpkin, acorn, kabocha), peeled, seeded and sliced into 2-inch (5-cm) slices

⅔ cup (5 oz/155 g) brown sugar

Preheat the oven to 375°F (190°C). Toss the ingredients together on a baking sheet, cover with foil, and roast for 20–30 minutes until soft. Let the squash cool, then purée in a blender, adding water if the purée is too thick. Chill for 7–10 days

SPICED PERSIMMON PURÉE

MAKES 1–2 CUPS, DEPENDING ON THE SIZE OF THE PERSIMMONS

2 very ripe persimmons, peeled and chopped

1 teaspoon ground cinnamon

¼ teaspoon ground cloves

1 teaspoon maple syrup

Place all ingredients in a blender and purée. Chill for 7–10 days.

CHERRY ICE CUBES

MAKES 6 LARGE ICE CUBES

1 cup (250 ml) tart cherry juice

6 frozen or fresh cherries, pitted

In a large liquid-measuring cup, stir together the cherry juice and 1 cup (250 ml) of water. Pour into 6 large ice-cube molds. Add 1 cherry to each mold and freeze overnight or for up to 3 months.

INDEX

A

Absinthe
    Classic Sazerac, 45
    London Cocktail, 22
    Pomme d'Amour, 102
    Sparkling Corpse Reviver, 100
Acai juice
    Mock Sangria, 168
Allspice Simple Syrup, 176
Amaretto Sour, 87
Americano, 92
Ancho Mezcalita, 67
Aperol
    Rhubarb Shrub, 42
Apple juice. *See also* Cider
    Apple Ginger Whiskey Sour, 110
Apples
    Apple & Honey Bee's Knees, 95
    Apple Hot Toddy, 152
    Cardamom Apple Pie, 107
    Highland Holiday Cocktail, 145
    Turmeric, Apple & Ginger Chai, 148
Arnold Palmer, Spiked, 75

B

Baileys Irish Cream
    Salted Caramel Irish Coffee, 170
Baltimore Eggnog, 124
Bar spoon, 10
Bar staples, 9
Bartender terms and techniques
    back, 16
    call, 16
    dry, 16
    flame, 16
    floating, or layering, note about, 128
    long, 16
    neat, 16
    (on the) rocks, 16
    twist, 16
    up, 16
    well/rail liquor, 16
Bar tools, 10–11

Basil
    Basil Julep, 51
    Basil Simple Syrup, 176
    Cucumber-Basil Gimlet, 166
    Nine-Botanical Bramble, 80
    Peach-Basil Mimosa, 56
    Peach-Basil Syrup, 176
    Strawberry Basil Gin & Tonic, 46
Beer
    Beer Margarita, 83
    Black Velvet, 137
    Bourbon Maple Fizz, 98
    Grapefruit Beer Bellini, 47
    Michelada, 169
    Morning Glory, 81
    Stout Sangaree, 130
Beets
    Mamacita (Mezcal Side Car), 117
Bellinis
    Blackberry-Thyme Bellini, 28
    Grapefruit Beer Bellini, 47
Benedictine liqueur
    Brandy Lift, 136
Berries. *See also specific berries*
    Champagne Cobbler, 54
    Fruit Shrubs, 178–79
    Pineapple Julep, 69
Blackberries
    Blackberry Lemonade Whiskey Sour, 57
    Blackberry-Thyme Bellini, 28
    Blackberry-Thyme Syrup, 176
    Mamacita (Mezcal Side Car), 117
    Mulled Winter Punch, 138
    Nine-Botanical Bramble, 80
Blackcurrant juice
    Mulled Winter Punch, 138
Black Russian, 170
Black Velvet, 137
Blood Orange Cosmopolitan, 167
Blood Orange Tequila Tropi-Cal, 105
Bloody Maria with Mezcal, 159
Bloody Mary, 157
Boston Shaker, 10

The Boulevardier, 96
Bourbon
    Amaretto Sour, 87
    Apple-Bourbon Hot Toddy, 153
    Basil Julep, 51
    The Boulevardier, 96
    Bourbon & Coffee Cocktail, 144
    Bourbon Maple Fizz, 98
    In Full Fig, 103
    Good Morning Grey, 118
    Mint Julep, 50
    Vanilla-Citrus Old-Fashioned, 149
Brandy
    Baltimore Eggnog, 124
    Brandied Mocha Coffee, 112
    Brandy Alexander, 160
    Brandy Crusta, 38
    Brandy Lift, 136
    Caffè Corretto, 146
    Chai-Spiced Hot Toddy, 115
    Coffee Cocktail, 140
    Metropole, 174
    Songbird, 23
    Tea Punch, 97
    Tom & Jerry, 131
Butter
    Hot Buttered Rum, 132
    Hot Buttered Yum, 133
    Salted Caramel, 178

C

Caffè Corretto, 146
Calvados
    Apple Hot Toddy, 152
    Pomme d'Amour, 102
Campari
    Americano, 92
    The Boulevardier, 96
    Classic Negroni, 161
    Frozen Orange Negroni, 161
    Oaxacan Negroni, 162
    Solstice Spritz, 72
    Tarragon Negroni, 162
Cappelletti
    The Hummingbird, 70
Caramel
    Salted Caramel, 178
    Salted Caramel Coffee, 109

    Salted Caramel Irish Coffee, 170
Cardamom Apple Pie, 107
Carrot, Ginger & Tequila Punch, 86
Chai, Turmeric, Apple & Ginger, 148
Chai-Spiced Hot Toddy, 115
Champagne Cobbler, 54
Champagne flute, 11
Channel knife, 10
Chartreuse
    Lemongrass Last Word, 65
    Songbird, 23
Cherries
    Cherry Ice Cubes, 181
    Hibiscus & Tart Cherry Manhattan, 160
    Metropole, 174
Chile liqueur
    Ancho Mezcalita, 67
    Mexican Hot Chocolate, 150
Chiles
    Spicy Yuzu Fizz, 74
    Tequila Sunrise with Pineapple & Jalapeño, 62
Chocolate
    Brandied Mocha Coffee, 112
    Hot Chocolate & Peppermint Schnapps, 147
    Mexican Hot Chocolate, 150
    Peanut Butter & Whiskey Milkshake, 79
    Salted Caramel Coffee, 109
    Spiked Peppermint Bark Hot Chocolate, 155
Cider
    Apple-Bourbon Hot Toddy, 153
    Cardamom Apple Pie, 107
    Cinnamon-Apple Syrup, 180
    Highland Holiday Cocktail, 145
    Pomegranate Apple Spiced Cider, 90
    Smoky Pumpkin, 106
Cinnamon
    Apple & Honey Bee's Knees, 95
    Cinnamon-Apple Syrup, 180
    Cinnamon Simple Syrup, 176
    Gingerbread Simple Syrup, 176
    Hot Buttered Yum, 133
    Persimmon Cinnamon Tea, 108
    Rum-Spiked Horchata, 76
    Winter Spiced Hibiscus, 143
Citrus & Spiced Mulled Wine, 139
Classic Negroni, 161
Classic Paloma, 129
Classic Sazerac, 45

Clover Club, 68
Cobbler, Champagne, 54
Cobbler Shaker, 10
Coconut
    Coconut Cream & Lime Margarita, 48
    Piña Colada, 170
Coffee
    Brandied Mocha Coffee, 112
    Caffè Corretto, 146
    Coffee Cocktail, 140
    Ice Coffee Mocktail, 141
    Irish Coffee, 169
    Salted Caramel Coffee, 109
    Salted Caramel Irish Coffee, 170
Coffee liqueur
    Black Russian, 170
    Bourbon & Coffee Cocktail, 144
    Peppermint White Russian, 171
    White Russian, 171
Coffee tincture
    The Hummingbird, 70
Cognac
    Baltimore Eggnog, 124
    Brandy Lift, 136
    Metropole, 174
Cointreau
    Beer Margarita, 83
    Blood Orange Cosmopolitan, 167
    Coconut Cream & Lime Margarita, 48
    Pegu Cocktail, 25
    Sparkling Corpse Reviver, 100
Collins glass, 11
Conifer needles
    Pining Away, 134
Copper mug, 11
Corpse Reviver, Sparkling, 100
Cosmopolitans
    Blood Orange Cosmopolitan, 167
    Cosmopolitan, 166–67
Coupe glass, 11
Cranberry juice
    Cosmopolitan, 166–67
Cream
    Brandy Alexander, 160
    Brandy Lift, 136
    Coffee Cocktail, 140
    Fresh Whipped Cream, 179
    Grasshopper, 175

    Irish Coffee, 169
    Peppermint White Russian, 171
    Ramos Gin Fizz, 174
    Salted Caramel, 178
    White Russian, 171
Cream of coconut
    Piña Colada, 170
Crème de cacao
    Brandy Alexander, 160
    Grasshopper, 175
Crème de cassis
    Kir Royal, 113
Crème de menthe
    Grasshopper, 175
Crème de mûre
    Nine-Botanical Bramble, 80
Cucumbers
    Cucumber-Basil Gimlet, 166
    Cucumber Elderflower Fizz, 43
    Morning Glory, 81
Curaçao
    Brandy Crusta, 38
    Mai Tai, 44
    Mamacita (Mezcal Side Car), 117
Cynar
    Songbird, 23

D

Daiquiris
    Daiquiri, 156
    note about, 156
    Raspberry-Peach Frozen Daiquiri, 156–57
    Thai Daiquiri, 157
Dark & Stormy, Gingerbread, 127
Dirty Martini, 172
Dry Martini, 171

E

Eggnog
    Baltimore Eggnog, 124
    Persimmon Nog, 125
Eggs
    Baltimore Eggnog, 124
    Persimmon Nog, 125
    Sherry Flip, 93
    Tom & Jerry, 131
Egg whites
    Amaretto Sour, 87

Apple Ginger Whiskey Sour, 110
Blackberry Lemonade Whiskey Sour, 57
Clover Club, 68
In Full Fig, 103
Mezcal Sour, 119
Ramos Gin Fizz, 174
El Chupacabra, 34
Elderflower liqueur
St-Germain Greyhound, 20
Sunset in the Garden, 114
Watermelon Tequila Punch, 84
Elderflower syrup
Cucumber Elderflower Fizz, 43
Spicy Yuzu Fizz, 74
Espresso
Caffè Corretto, 146

F

Faux-Loma, 30
Figs
In Full Fig, 103
The Final Four, 27
Fresh Lemonade, 180
Fresh Whipped Cream, 179
Frozen Orange Negroni, 161
Fruit. *See also specific fruits*
Fruit Shrubs, 178–79

G

Garnishes, 14
Genever
Pineapple Julep, 69
Gimlets
Cucumber-Basil Gimlet, 166
Gimlet, 165
Grapefruit & Sage Gimlet, 166
Gin
Apple & Honey Bee's Knees, 95
Classic Negroni, 161
Clover Club, 68
Dry Martini, 171
Frozen Orange Negroni, 161
Gimlet, 165
Ginger Gin Rickey, 33
Grapefruit & Sage Gimlet, 166
Flipped Martini, 172
Lemongrass Last Word, 65
London Cocktail, 22

Pegu Cocktail, 25
Ramos Gin Fizz, 174
Raspberry Gin Fizz, 60
Rhubarb Spritz, 41
Rosé and Roses, 36
Sparkling Corpse Reviver, 100
The Spring Solar, 35
Strawberry Basil Gin & Tonic, 46
Tarragon Negroni, 162
Ginger
Apple Ginger Whiskey Sour, 110
Carrot, Ginger & Tequila Punch, 86
Chai-Spiced Hot Toddy, 115
Gingerbread Dark & Stormy, 127
Gingerbread Simple Syrup, 176
Ginger Gin Rickey, 33
Ginger Simple Syrup, 176
Persimmon Cinnamon Tea, 108
Rosemary-Ginger Mojito, 165
Rosemary-Ginger Simple Syrup, 176
Turmeric, Apple & Ginger Chai, 148
Warming Milk, 151
Winter Spiced Hibiscus, 143
Ginger ale
Mock Mojito, 163
Summer Cup, 61
Ginger beer
Gingerbread Dark & Stormy, 127
Saint Tiki, 59
Wild Mule, 122
Gingerbread Dark & Stormy, 127
Good Morning Grey, 118
Grapefruit beer
Grapefruit Beer Bellini, 47
Grapefruit & grapefruit juice
Classic Paloma, 129
El Chupacabra, 34
Faux-Loma, 30
Grapefruit Beer Bellini, 47
Grapefruit & Sage Gimlet, 166
St-Germain Greyhound, 20
Sunset in the Garden, 114
Grape juice
Mock Sangria, 168
Not Your Negroni, 161
Grasshopper, 175
Grenadine
Lychee & Lime Sake Cocktail, 64

Tequila Sunrise with Pineapple & Jalapeño, 62
Guar gum, note about, 38

H

Hawthorne Strainer, 11
Herbsaint
  Classic Sazerac, 45
Hibiscus
  Hibiscus Simple Syrup, 176
  Hibiscus & Tart Cherry Manhattan, 160
  Winter Spiced Hibiscus, 143
Highball, 11
Highland Holiday Cocktail, 145
Honey
  Cinnamon-Apple Syrup, 180
  Honeybee Fizz, 82
Horchata, Rum-Spiked, 76
Hot Buttered Rum, 132
Hot Buttered Yum, 133
Hot chocolate
  Hot Chocolate & Peppermint Schnapps, 147
  Mexican Hot Chocolate, 150
  Spiked Peppermint Bark Hot Chocolate, 155
Hot toddies
  Apple-Bourbon Hot Toddy, 153
  Apple Hot Toddy, 152
  Chai-Spiced Hot Toddy, 115
The Hummingbird, 70

I

Ice, 13
Ice Coffee Mocktail, 141
Ice cream
  Hot Buttered Yum, 133
  Peanut Butter & Whiskey Milkshake, 79
Ice Cubes, Cherry, 181
In Full Fig, 103
Irish Coffee, 169

J

Jigger, 10
Juicers, 10
Julep cup, 11
Juleps
  Basil Julep, 51
  Mint Julep, 50
  note about, 50
  Pineapple Julep, 69

Julep Strainer, 11
Flipped Martini, 172

K

Kaffir lime leaves
  Lemongrass Last Word, 65
  Thai Daiquiri, 157
Kaffir Lime & Rosemary Oleo Saccharum, 179
Kahlua
  Peppermint White Russian, 171
Kir Royal, 113

L

Lemonade
  Fresh Lemonade, 180
  Spiked Arnold Palmer, 75
Lemongrass
  Lemongrass Last Word, 65
  Lemongrass Simple Syrup, 176
Lemons & lemon juice
  Blackberry Lemonade Whiskey Sour, 57
  Fresh Lemonade, 180
  Honeybee Fizz, 82
  New York Sour, 128
  Vanilla-Citrus Old-Fashioned, 149
Lillet
  Sparkling Corpse Reviver, 100
  Strawberry-Lillet Vodka Soda, 39
Lillet Blanc
  Tarragon Negroni, 162
Lillet Rosé
  Rosita Spritz, 31
Limes & lime juice
  Basil Julep, 51
  Coconut Cream & Lime Margarita, 48
  Cosmopolitan, 166–67
  Daiquiri, 156
  Faux-Loma, 30
  Gimlet, 165
  Lemongrass Last Word, 65
  Lychee & Lime Sake Cocktail, 64
  Margarita, 162
  Mock Mojito, 163
  Mojito, 163
  Raspberry Gin Fizz, 60
  Rosemary-Ginger Mojito, 165
  Thai Daiquiri, 157
  Watermelon Juice, 71

Wild Mule, 122
London Cocktail, 22
Lychee & Lime Sake Cocktail, 64

M

Madeira
    Baltimore Eggnog, 124
Mai Tai, 44
Mamacita (Mezcal Side Car), 117
Manhattans
    Hibiscus & Tart Cherry Manhattan, 160
    Manhattan, 160
    Scotch Manhattan, 101
Maple syrup
    Bourbon Maple Fizz, 98
    Cardamom Apple Pie, 107
    Highland Holiday Cocktail, 145
    Persimmon Nog, 125
    Pining Away, 134
    Smoky Pumpkin, 106
Maraschino liqueur
    Pineapple Julep, 69
Margaritas
    Beer Margarita, 83
    Coconut Cream & Lime Margarita, 48
    Margarita, 162
Martini glass, 11
Martinis
    Dirty Martini, 172
    Dry Martini, 171
    Flipped Martini, 172
A Meadow for Eeyore, 26
Metropole, 174
Mexican Hot Chocolate, 150
Mezcal. See also Tequila
    Ancho Mezcalita, 67
    Bloody Maria with Mezcal, 159
    El Chupacabra, 34
    Mamacita (Mezcal Side Car), 117
    Mezcal Sour, 119
    Morning Glory, 81
    Nine-Botanical Bramble, 80
    Oaxacan Negroni, 162
    Rosita Spritz, 31
    Smooth Criminal, 77
    The Spring Solar, 35
    Sunset in the Garden, 114
Michelada, 169

Milk
    Baltimore Eggnog, 124
    Brandied Mocha Coffee, 112
    Hot Chocolate & Peppermint Schnapps, 147
    Mexican Hot Chocolate, 150
    Peanut Butter & Whiskey Milkshake, 79
    Persimmon Nog, 125
    Pining Away, 134
    Salted Caramel Coffee, 109
    Spiked Peppermint Bark Hot Chocolate, 155
    Tom & Jerry, 131
    Warming Milk, 151
Milkshake, Peanut Butter & Whiskey, 79
Mimosa, Peach-Basil, 56
Mint
    Mint Julep, 50
    Mock Mojito, 163
    Mojito, 163
Mixers, 9
Mocha Coffee, Brandied, 112
Mock Mojito, 163
Mock Sangria, 168
Mojitos
    Mock Mojito, 163
    Mojito, 163
    Rosemary-Ginger Mojito, 165
Morning Glory, 81
Muddler, 10
Mulled Wine, Citrus & Spiced, 139
Mulled Winter Punch, 138

N

Negronis
    Classic Negroni, 161
    Frozen Orange Negroni, 161
    Not Your Negroni, 161
    Oaxacan Negroni, 162
    Tarragon Negroni, 162
New York Sour, 128
Nine-Botanical Bramble, 80
Nonalcoholic drinks
    Cardamom Apple Pie, 107
    Cucumber-Basil Gimlet, 166
    Cucumber Elderflower Fizz, 43
    Faux-Loma, 30
    Honeybee Fizz, 82
    Hot Buttered Yum, 133
    Ice Coffee Mocktail, 141

Mexican Hot Chocolate, 150
Mock Mojito, 163
Mock Sangria, 168
Mulled Winter Punch, 138
Not Your Negroni, 161
Persimmon Cinnamon Tea, 108
Persimmon Nog, 125
Piña Colada, 170
Pining Away, 134
Pomegranate Apple Spiced Cider, 90
Saint Tiki, 59
Smoky Pumpkin, 106
Turmeric, Apple & Ginger Chai, 148
Warming Milk, 151
Watermelon Juice, 71
Wild Mule, 122
Winter Spiced Hibiscus, 143
Not Your Negroni, 161

O

Oaxacan Negroni, 162
Old-Fashioned, 159
Old-Fashioned, Vanilla-Citrus, 149
Oleo Saccharum, Kaffir Lime & Rosemary, 179
Olives
    Dirty Martini, 172
    Dry Martini, 171
Orange liqueur
    Brandy Crusta, 38
    Cosmopolitan, 166–67
    Mai Tai, 44
    Mamacita (Mezcal Side Car), 117
    Margarita, 162
    Sangria, 167
    Solstice Spritz, 72
Oranges & orange juice
    Blood Orange Cosmopolitan, 167
    Blood Orange Tequila Tropi-Cal, 105
    Carrot, Ginger & Tequila Punch, 86
    Chai-Spiced Hot Toddy, 115
    Citrus & Spiced Mulled Wine, 139
    Frozen Orange Negroni, 161
    Ice Coffee Mocktail, 141
    Mock Sangria, 168
    Mulled Winter Punch, 138
    Not Your Negroni, 161
    Pineapple Julep, 69
    Saint Tiki, 59

Tequila Sunrise with Pineapple & Jalapeño, 62
Triple Orange Tincture, 179–80
Vanilla-Citrus Old-Fashioned, 149
Orange tincture
    The Final Four, 27
    Triple Orange Tincture, 179–80
Orgeat
    Brandy Lift, 136
    Mai Tai, 44

P

Paloma, Classic, 129
Peaches
    Peach-Basil Mimosa, 56
    Peach-Basil Syrup, 176
    Raspberry-Peach Frozen Daiquiri, 156–57
    Rosé & Peach Sangria, 168
    Smooth Criminal, 77
Peanut Butter & Whiskey Milkshake, 79
Pegu Cocktail, 25
Peppermint Bark Hot Chocolate, Spiked, 155
Peppermint schnapps
    Hot Chocolate & Peppermint Schnapps, 147
    Peppermint White Russian, 171
Persimmons
    Persimmon Cinnamon Tea, 108
    Persimmon Nog, 125
    Spiced Persimmon Purée, 181
Pimm's No.1
    Summer Cup, 61
Piña Colada, 170
Pineapple & pineapple juice
    Blood Orange Tequila Tropi-Cal, 105
    Piña Colada, 170
    Pineapple Julep, 69
    Saint Tiki, 59
    Tequila Sunrise with Pineapple & Jalapeño, 62
Pining Away, 134
Pomegranate
    Mulled Winter Punch, 138
    Pomegranate Apple Spiced Cider, 90
Pomme d'Amour, 102
Port
    Stout Sangaree, 130
Pumpkin
    Smoky Pumpkin, 106
    Winter Squash Purée, 180
Punch

Carrot, Ginger & Tequila Punch, 86
Mulled Winter Punch, 138
Pineapple Julep, 69
Tea Punch, 97
Watermelon Tequila Punch, 84
Punch bowl, 11

R

Ramos Gin Fizz, 174
Raspberries
Raspberry Gin Fizz, 60
Raspberry-Peach Frozen Daiquiri, 156–57
Rosé & Peach Sangria, 168
Raspberry simple syrup
Clover Club, 68
Pineapple Julep, 69
Raspberry Gin Fizz, 60
Raspberry Simple Syrup, 176
Rhubarb
Rhubarb Shrub, 42
Rhubarb Spritz, 41
Rhubarb Syrup, 178
Rice
Rum-Spiked Horchata, 76
Rich Simple Syrup, 176
Rocks glass, 11
Rosé and Roses, 36
Rosemary
Kaffir Lime & Rosemary Oleo Saccharum, 179
Rosemary-Ginger Mojito, 165
Rosemary-Ginger Simple Syrup, 176
Rosé & Peach Sangria, 168
Rose water
Rosé and Roses, 36
Rosita Spritz, 31
Rum
Baltimore Eggnog, 124
Chai-Spiced Hot Toddy, 115
Daiquiri, 156
Gingerbread Dark & Stormy, 127
Hot Buttered Rum, 132
Mai Tai, 44
Mojito, 163
Raspberry-Peach Frozen Daiquiri, 156–57
Rosemary-Ginger Mojito, 165
Rum-Spiked Horchata, 76
Salted Caramel Coffee, 109
Tea Punch, 97

Tom & Jerry, 131
Rye whiskey
Classic Sazerac, 45
Manhattan, 160
Pomme d'Amour, 102

S

Sage
Grapefruit & Sage Gimlet, 166
Sage Simple Syrup, 176
Saint Tiki, 59
Sake Cocktail, Lychee & Lime, 64
Salted Caramel, 178
Salted Caramel Coffee, 109
Salted Caramel Irish Coffee, 170
Sanbitter
Not Your Negroni, 161
Sangaree, Stout, 130
Sangria
Mock Sangria, 168
Rosé & Peach Sangria, 168
Sangria, 167
Sazerac, Classic, 45
Scotch
Highland Holiday Cocktail, 145
Scotch Manhattan, 101
Shakers, 10
Sherry Flip, 93
Shrubs
Fruit Shrubs, 178–79
Rhubarb Shrub, 42
Simple syrups
Allspice Simple Syrup, 176
Basil Simple Syrup, 176
Cinnamon Simple Syrup, 176
Gingerbread Simple Syrup, 176
Ginger Simple Syrup, 176
Hibiscus Simple Syrup, 176
Lemongrass Simple Syrup, 176
Raspberry Simple Syrup, 176
Rich Simple Syrup, 176
Rosemary-Ginger Simple Syrup, 176
Sage Simple Syrup, 176
Simple Syrup, 176
Tarragon Simple Syrup, 176
Thyme Simple Syrup, 176
Vanilla Simple Syrup, 176
Smoky Pumpkin, 106

Smooth Criminal, 77
Sodas, 9
Solstice Spritz, 72
Songbird, 23
Sparkling Corpse Reviver, 100
Sparkling wine
    Blackberry-Thyme Bellini, 28
    Black Velvet, 137
    Champagne Cobbler, 54
    Kir Royal, 113
    Peach-Basil Mimosa, 56
    Pineapple Julep, 69
    Rhubarb Spritz, 41
    Rosé and Roses, 36
    Rosita Spritz, 31
    Solstice Spritz, 72
    Sunset in the Garden, 114
Spiced Persimmon Purée, 181
Spicy Yuzu Fizz, 74
Spiked Arnold Palmer, 75
Spiked Peppermint Bark Hot Chocolate, 155
The Spring Solar, 35
Squash
    Smoky Pumpkin, 106
    Winter Squash Purée, 180
St-Germain
    St-Germain Greyhound, 20
    Sunset in the Garden, 114
    Watermelon Tequila Punch, 84
Stout
    Black Velvet, 137
    Bourbon Maple Fizz, 98
    Stout Sangaree, 130
Strainers, 10–11
Strawberries
    Mock Sangria, 168
    Rhubarb Shrub, 42
    Rosé and Roses, 36
    Strawberry Basil Gin & Tonic, 46
    Strawberry-Lillet Vodka Soda, 39
Summer Cup, 61
Sunset in the Garden, 114
Syrups
    Allspice Simple Syrup, 176
    Basil Simple Syrup, 176
    Blackberry-Thyme Syrup, 176
    Cinnamon-Apple Syrup, 180
    Cinnamon Simple Syrup, 176

Gingerbread Simple Syrup, 176
    Ginger Simple Syrup, 176
    Hibiscus Simple Syrup, 176
    Lemongrass Simple Syrup, 176
    Peach-Basil Syrup, 176
    Raspberry Simple Syrup, 176
    Rhubarb Syrup, 178
    Rich Simple Syrup, 176
    Rosemary-Ginger Simple Syrup, 176
    Sage Simple Syrup, 176
    Simple Syrup, 176
    Tarragon Simple Syrup, 176
    Thyme Simple Syrup, 176
    Vanilla Simple Syrup, 176

T
Tarragon
    Tarragon Negroni, 162
    Tarragon Simple Syrup, 176
Tea
    Chai-Spiced Hot Toddy, 115
    Good Morning Grey, 118
    Persimmon Cinnamon Tea, 108
    Smoky Pumpkin, 106
    Spicy Yuzu Fizz, 74
    Spiked Arnold Palmer, 75
    Tea Punch, 97
    Turmeric, Apple & Ginger Chai, 148
Tequila
    Beer Margarita, 83
    Blood Orange Tequila Tropi-Cal, 105
    Carrot, Ginger & Tequila Punch, 86
    Classic Paloma, 129
    Coconut Cream & Lime Margarita, 48
    Margarita, 162
    Mexican Hot Chocolate, 150
    Rosé and Roses, 36
    Tequila Sunrise with Pineapple & Jalapeño, 62
    Watermelon Tequila Punch, 84
Thai Daiquiri, 157
Thyme
    Blackberry-Thyme Bellini, 28
    Blackberry-Thyme Syrup, 176
    Thyme Simple Syrup, 176
Tinctures
    preparing, note about, 26
    Triple Orange Tincture, 179–80
Tomato juice

Bloody Maria with Mezcal, 159
Bloody Mary, 157
Michelada, 169
Tom & Jerry, 131
Triple Orange Tincture, 179–80
Triple sec
    Brandy Crusta, 38
    Cosmopolitan, 166–67
    Mamacita (Mezcal Side Car), 117
    Margarita, 162
    Solstice Spritz, 72
Turmeric
    Turmeric, Apple & Ginger Chai, 148
    Warming Milk, 151

V

Vanilla-Citrus Old-Fashioned, 149
Vanilla Simple Syrup, 176
Vermouth
    Americano, 92
    The Boulevardier, 96
    Classic Negroni, 161
    Clover Club, 68
    Dirty Martini, 172
    Dry Martini, 171
    The Final Four, 27
    Frozen Orange Negroni, 161
    Hibiscus & Tart Cherry Manhattan, 160
    Flipped Martini, 172
    Manhattan, 160
    A Meadow for Eeyore, 26
    Metropole, 174
    Oaxacan Negroni, 162
    Rhubarb Shrub, 42
    Rhubarb Spritz, 41
    Scotch Manhattan, 101
Vinegar
    Fruit Shrubs, 178–79
Vodka
    Black Russian, 170
    Blood Orange Cosmopolitan, 167
    Bloody Mary, 157
    Cosmopolitan, 166–67
    Dirty Martini, 172
    The Final Four, 27
    Peppermint White Russian, 171
    preparing tinctures with, 26
    Rosé and Roses, 36

Rosé & Peach Sangria, 168
Spiked Arnold Palmer, 75
Spiked Peppermint Bark Hot Chocolate, 155
St-Germain Greyhound, 20
Strawberry-Lillet Vodka Soda, 39
Triple Orange Tincture, 179–80
White Russian, 171

W

Warming Milk, 151
Watermelon
    Watermelon Juice, 71
    Watermelon Tequila Punch, 84
Whipped Cream, Fresh, 179
Whiskey
    Apple Ginger Whiskey Sour, 110
    Blackberry Lemonade Whiskey Sour, 57
    Chai-Spiced Hot Toddy, 115
    Hibiscus & Tart Cherry Manhattan, 160
    Irish Coffee, 169
    New York Sour, 128
    Old-Fashioned, 159
    Peanut Butter & Whiskey Milkshake, 79
    Persimmon Cinnamon Tea, 108
White Russian, 171
White Russian, Peppermint, 171
Wild Mule, 122
Wine. See also Sparkling wine
    Citrus & Spiced Mulled Wine, 139
    New York Sour, 128
    Rosé & Peach Sangria, 168
    Sangria, 167
    Stout Sangaree, 130
Winter Spiced Hibiscus, 143
Winter Squash Purée, 180

Y

Yuzu Fizz, Spicy, 74

DRINKS FOR EVERY SEASON

Conceived and produced by Weldon Owen International
in collaboration with Williams Sonoma, Inc.
3250 Van Ness Avenue, San Francisco, CA 94109

A WELDON OWEN PRODUCTION
PO Box 3088
San Rafael, CA 94912
www.weldonowen.com

WELDON OWEN INTERNATIONAL
CEO Raoul Goff
Publisher Roger Shaw
Associate Publisher Amy Marr
Managing Editor Katie Killebrew
Editorial Assistant Jourdan Plautz

Creative Director Chrissy Kwasnik
Designer Ali Ziegler
Production Manager Sam Taylor

Printed in China
10 9 8 7 6 5 4 3 2

Photographer Erin Scott
Food & Prop Stylist Jillian Knox
Food Styling on pages 9, 36, 59, 62, 79, 164
by Emily Caneer

Library of Congress
Cataloging-in-Publication data is available.

ISBN: 978-1-68188-778-4

Weldon Owen wishes to thank the following people
for their generous support in producing this book:
Lesley Bruynesteyn, Isabelle English, Devon Francis, and Elizabeth Parson